AMONG THE
GENTLY MAD

AMONG THE
GENTLY MAD

Perspectives and Strategies for the

Book Hunter in the Twenty-first Century

NICHOLAS A. BASBANES

A JOHN MACRAE BOOK

Henry Holt and Company | New York

Henry Holt and Company, LLC
Publishers since 1866
115 West 18th Street
New York, New York 10011

Henry Holt ® is a registered trademark of
Henry Holt and Company, LLC.

Library of Congress Cataloging-in-Publication Data
Basbanes, Nicholas A., 1943–
Among the gently mad : perspectives and strategies for the
book hunter in the twenty-first century / Nicholas A. Basbanes.
    p. cm.
"A John Macrae book."
Includes bibliographical references and index.
ISBN: 0-8050-5159-7
1. Book collecting. 2. Antiquarian booksellers.
3. Book collecting—Computer network resources. 4. Antiquarian
booksellers—Computer network resources.   I. Title.

Z987 .B28 2002
002'.075—dc21   2002066854

Henry Holt books are available for special
promotions and premiums. For details contact:
Director, Special Markets.

First Edition 2002

Designed by Paula Russell Szafranski

Printed in the United States of America

1   3   5   7   9   10   8   6   4   2

For Connie, Barbara, and Nicole,

the women in my life

As I look back, I am acutely conscious that every primary and priceless work of literature I have handled and studied in a library had originally been part of a private collection. Whether it was the packrat instinct or a fine humanistic passion that led the first collector to bring this book together with the others so that ultimately many works of scholarship were based on them is of no importance—the value to humanity is the same. And, I trust, so is the pleasure to the collector.

—Fredson Bowers,
First Printings of American Authors

CONTENTS

AMONG THE
GENTLY MAD

FIRST PRINCIPLES

The first documented use of the word *bibliomania* in English came in 1750 when Philip Dormer Stanhope, the fourth Earl of Chesterfield and a wily politician with a gift for turning a memorable phrase, sent a haughty letter to his illegitimate son, then away at school, to warn of a consuming diversion that should be avoided like the bubonic plague. "Buy good books, and read them," the lord advised the impressionable lad, urging him to choose the sanity of substance over what he felt was the senselessness of scarcity; "the best books are the commonest, and the last editions are always the best, if the editors are not blockheads." Several decades would pass before the term came to widespread prominence, and even then it was drolly described as a "fatal disease" by its most famous chronicler, a country clergyman named Thomas Frognall Dibdin whose insatiable passion for books led him to write a landmark tract on the subject, aptly titled *The Bibliomania.* The reverend's tongue-in-cheek diagnosis caused a minor sensation when it first appeared in 1809, and came to epitomize a good deal of the fervor then taking place in what became known as the Heroic Age of Book Collecting.

For all the notoriety the colorful term ultimately did acquire, however, the more genteel practitioners of this manic exercise preferred referring to themselves as book hunters, a seemingly respectable designation that offered a summary description of what they were up to in their idle time while hedging a bit on the more troubling matter of obsession. Perhaps the best-known champion of the alternate phrase was John Hill Burton, a nineteenth-century scholar from Edinburgh anointed the historiographer royal of Scotland in recognition of a three-volume history of his native land, but remembered largely today for a lively labor of love he temperately called *The Book-Hunter.* This good-humored overview of what Burton called the "disposition to possess books," first published in 1862, inspired a number of other authors to use the same designation, Octave Uzanne's *Book-Hunter in Paris* (1893), William Roberts's *Book-Hunter in London* (1895), and P. B. M. Allan's *Book-Hunter at Home* (1920) most notable among them. "The object of this rambling preamble is to win from the reader a morsel of genial fellow-feeling towards the human frailty which we are going to examine," Burton explained of his purpose, taking pains to point out that when compared to other personal habits, this "failing," as he waggishly put it, remains the one above all others "that leans to virtue's side." What he seemed to be suggesting is that despite all evidence to the contrary, collectors are *not* crazy people, or even fatally flawed for that matter, that there is in fact a method to their madness, one that involves, in an admittedly curious way, a gift of perception, albeit distinguished by an amusing paradox. "It is, as you will observe, the general ambition of the class to find value where there seems to be none, and this develops a certain skill and subtlety, enabling the operator, in the midst of a heap of rubbish, to put his finger on those things which have in them the latent capacity to become valuable and curious."

At no time in history have such skills become more useful than the present. We have entered an age, in fact, in which nothing is without value, an era when *everything*, it seems, is collectible. What has occasioned this newfound fascination for artifacts is anyone's guess, but it could well be due to renewed respect for the "real thing," particularly at a time when so much popular culture is coming to us in the zeros and ones of digital transmission. Whatever the reason, people are well advised to take a second look at old possessions that in other times might have been sent off for final disposition in the local landfill or put to the torch in the municipal incinerator.

In the twenty-five years or so that I have been actively moving among people I have affectionately chosen to call the gently mad, I have gathered a number of insights into these "latent capacities" people have to gather books from the unlikeliest of places. While my primary purpose in these investigations has been to understand the broader aspects of what we might call book culture, I have paid careful attention to how these individuals go about doing what they do, and I have adopted a number of their precepts for my own use as I go about my own hunt for books. While my intention in this effort is not to serve up a conventional guidebook to the mechanics of book collecting, since primers of that sort already exist in abundance, I do hope to offer a general commentary on the relevance of the exercise in a constantly changing world, spicing the narrative from time to time with a few of the views I have gathered along the way, some "tips from the pros," as it were, that might prove as interesting to the serious collector of rarities as they are instructive for the amateur just starting out. Keeping that qualification in mind, it might be useful to consider this modest effort a code of first principles developed and tested in the field, with the understanding that these are *my* first principles, and that readers should feel free to develop systems of their own. When I was visiting the monastic republic of Mount Athos on the Chalkidiki Peninsula of northern Greece in 1998 to learn what I could about the manuscript collections that have been maintained there for a thousand years, I ran across a lovely word, idiorhythmic, which describes a kind of relaxed monasticism no longer in favor in which adherents could more or less follow their own rules, not those of an inflexible abbot. Translated from the Greek, idiorhythmic means "living by one's own life patterns," and it suggests for me a way to go about the business of scouting out books.

Because my approach is decidedly personal and somewhat discursive, it may well be a good idea to emphasize that I am not a bookseller, I am not a librarian, I am not a professional bibliographer, and though I certainly do seek out books for pleasure, I by no means rank myself anywhere near the top tier of collectors, not even close. Indeed, it was an early realization that I would never own books that could possibly compare with the remarkable collections I was seeing as a literary journalist that contributed to my decision to write about some of the great book hunters past and present, to enjoy, if only in a vicarious way, treasures that I myself could never dream of owning. I was once introduced at a colloquium sponsored by the American Antiquarian Society as a "collector of collectors," and the truth is that I have developed something of a possessive attitude toward the people I have written about, regarding them as *my* collectors and *my* librarians, *my* booksellers and *my* archivists, which they are, in a sense, by virtue of the fact that all have allowed me to enter their lives and to share, if only for a few hours, the joy and the satisfaction of what they have accomplished. There is an added dimension to this: the fact that I truly regard what I do as a work-in-progress even after my books appear in print, that once granted access to the impassioned pursuits of these individuals, I feel an obligation to keep tabs on what they are doing, on *how* they are doing, and to report from time to time on the various ways they fit into the unending cycle of books and book people.

The enduring beauty of collecting books is that satisfaction is possible at every level of activity, and one of the very first rules I can offer is the same rule casino operators suggest that neophyte gamblers apply when making their first role of the dice or their first turn of a card, and that is to know your limits, to work within a budget, and above all else to play with your head, not your gut. The collector who is motivated by the prospect of making money is going at it for all the wrong reasons. It is true that good books bought wisely have proven to be solid investments over the years, but there is a wild card in the mix, and that is the fickle nature of fashion. Just ask what people who bought heavily in John Galsworthy fifty or sixty years ago paid for first edition copies of the three novels in his Forsyte saga series, and you will find the literary equivalent of Enron stock: a shrewd buy one day, not so shrewd the next. The fact that Galsworthy won a Nobel Prize in 1932 is a laudable accomplishment, but not nearly enough to justify outlandishly high prices for his books today, especially when so much of what he wrote about the upper middle class is dated and no longer popular among a general readership.

There is a flip side to this, and it brings to the fore a lesson I learned from the late Sanford L. Berger, arguably the greatest collector ever of material relating to the life and work of the English poet, designer, and bookmaker William Morris, and it involves what we might call a bite-the-bullet approach to whether or not collectors on a budget can afford to buy some marginal titles that are just on the cusp of their interests, and just beyond their available resources. "I have a nice list of should'ves, things I should have bought and didn't," he told me in 1990, using as his prime example the 1638 copy of a book known as Gerard's *Herbal,* which he was offered twenty-two years earlier but did not buy. By influencing many of the floral designs created by William Morris, the book was of peripheral importance to Berger's primary interest. "It was three hundred dollars and I didn't get it because in 1968 I was focusing only on Kelmscott Press items. Now that I'm deep into the decorative arts, I realize how nice it would be to have that book." The only problem was that every time Berger saw a copy listed in a catalog, the price was always more than he was willing to pay at the time, with listings running around four thousand dollars when we spoke. "I don't care to have it that much. But I *should've* bought it for three hundred when I had the chance."

On a much more modest scale, I keep telling myself that sooner or later *The Carpentered Hen* (1958), John Updike's first published book—a volume of poetry—and *Goodbye, Columbus,* the debut work of short fiction by Philip Roth, which won a National Book Award for fiction in 1960, will come my way, and that with those two acquisitions I will at long last finish off my runs of those authors. But as the years go by, and as the prices for these books keep spiraling upward, the chances of that happening keep getting slimmer and slimmer, and every now and then I realize that maybe I, too, *should've* bought them not so long ago when they were priced at a couple of hundred dollars each, not the eight hundred and fifty dollars I would have to fork out today for the Updike, or the fifteen hundred dollars that would be necessary to secure a fine copy of the Roth.

There is another conviction that applies in this regard, one articulated by Walter L. Pforzheimer, a former senior officer with the Central Intelligence Agency and collector of what is regarded as the most comprehensive "spy" collection in the world. Pforzheimer told me that he became a serious collector one day in 1950 when he was in New York on agency business and walked into Scribner's bookstore on Fifth Avenue to look around. "I had been getting relevant things along the way, but they were to read, not collect," he recalled. But when he was shown a letter in George Washington's hand advocating the "necessities of procuring good Intelligence," he knew he had a momentous decision to make. "We are now at the make or break point. Do you or don't you collect? I had not considered myself a collector of intelligence material until I was faced with this document, and what do you do? Well, there's no question of what you do; you just cannot let something like that go by."

On a related plane, I realize that it is probably a little late in the day for me to start collecting some of the fresh new voices that are announcing their arrival on the literary scene with an eye toward running the table on their published works, the most obvious reason being the likelihood that they will still be writing books long after I have turned over my last page. But it is kind of fun, all the same, to handicap authors that I believe will be winners over the long haul, to take a chance on, in a manner of speaking, extended growth. I would have to rank among my more sagacious "picks" my decision to get in on the ground floor with the fiction writers Louise Erdrich, Howard Norman, Sue Miller, Ethan Canin, Brad Leithauser, Bobbie Ann Mason, Jayne Ann Phillips, Allan Gurganus, and Kazuo Ishiguro, and to have followed their fortunes from the very start of their careers, beginning at a time when their names were unknown outside of their inner circles. A tip from Irwin T. Holtzman, one of the more enterprising collectors of modern first editions over the past forty years, is one I have followed with some rigor, and that is to pay attention to the early reviews in *Publishers Weekly, Library Journal, Booklist,* and *Kirkus,* trade magazines that now maintain active websites and are available for general reference in the periodical rooms of most libraries. These concise forecasts typically come out several months ahead of official release dates, and if you have a mind toward getting sets of the bound galleys or what more recently have been called advance reader copies or ARCs, this is the time to act, not later, when the whole world is onto the author, and everyone else is beseeching dealers for sets of the uncorrected proofs.

Reviews certainly should never be treated as the final word, but they are a valid indicator of incipient talent, especially if the critic is someone whose work you know and respect. I am less likely to be swayed by the opinions of other critics, and will not let their opinions influence my judgment one way or the other. Of singular importance here is the necessity of keeping an open mind. Do not let reviewers push you around or intimidate you with their fancy footwork. If the author is somebody you like, and somebody you want to collect, then it's your dime, and another one of Holtzman's points—that he collected authors, not just books, and that fully 40 percent of the first editions he acquired were bought at the time of publication, and therefore at the publisher's list price—is worth heeding as well. Essentially, what we are talking about here is that elusive quality known as *literary merit,* but even that, as we all know, is an ambiguous attribute that is subject to constant change. To appreciate the point, one need only consider what Thomas Bailey Aldrich wrote in the *Atlantic Monthly* in 1892 about the posthumously published poems of Emily Dickinson. "An eccentric, dreamy, half-educated recluse in an out-of-the-way New England village," he declared. "Oblivion lingers in the immediate neighborhood." If that seems a bit too dated, consider what Whitney Balliett had to say in the *New Yorker* in 1961 about Joseph Heller's *Catch-22:* "Heller wallows in his own laughter and finally drowns in it. What remains is a debris of sour jokes, stage anger, dirty words, synthetic looniness, and the sort of antic behavior the children fall into when they know they are losing our attention."

On the advisability of collecting what have become known as hypermoderns, or books that are being declared collectible simultaneous with their release to the general trade, the advice from here is to be careful, and to consider, exactly, who is saying that a book just published is a sure bet to double or triple in value six months from now, a year from now, ten years from now. I by no means say that serious collectors should stay away from this sort of speculation; in fact, like Holtzman, I encourage readers to buy first edition copies of works by their favorite authors as they arrive in print, but they should pay no more than the listed retail price at the time of publication. "For me, the idea is to get it fresh off the press," Holtzman said. "I am partial to the living, to the future. I can always pick up what was written yesterday. I am more interested in what will be published tomorrow. I think that is the challenge of being a contemporary collector." In addition to selecting new works as they appear in print, it is worth noting that remainder tables offering books at less than retail have their moments too, though it is especially important to check the copyright pages and make sure that they are first editions. This rule, of course, applies in every first encounter with a book being considered for acquisition, and it behooves beginners to go about this task efficiently. As the noted author, bibliographer, and collector Matthew J. Bruccoli has written, "Knowing how to identify the first publication of a book is essential to book collecting and bibliographical research." I direct those who need help in this area to my selected bibliography in the Appendix.

For young collectors just starting out and inclined toward newly released fiction, I suggest getting books by authors you believe you will feel comfortable maturing with, and that you build around them as you go along. The books that I have the greatest affection for comprise what I call my Authors I Grew Up With Collection, the books that began to captivate me as a young adult and helped shape my view of the world as I made my way through life. Thus it should come as no surprise to anyone who knows my tastes in fiction that I have respectable first edition collections of John Steinbeck, William Faulkner, Ernest Hemingway, and Thomas Wolfe, standard readings of my early years. As an undergraduate English major at Bates College in the early 1960s, an awakening appreciation for reading what I describe as performance literature has resulted in the assembly of complete runs in first edition of the plays of Tennessee Williams and Arthur Miller. Sadly, my shelves do not include the corpus of F. Scott Fitzgerald, not because I don't want him represented there, but because first issue copies of his books have always been beyond my financial means. One group of books that I have had the greatest fun assembling—and which have cost me next to nothing—is what I call my Orphan Collection, so named because it is composed entirely of perfectly wonderful books that have been discarded over the years by various libraries as either out of scope or out of fashion, and therefore have been deemed expendable. Because all are ex libris volumes, each one bears a bookplate indicating prior ownership at one institution or another, and all have the notation "withdrawn" or "discard" stamped or written inside. It is the literary equivalent of going to the animal pound and giving a stray dog faced with an uncertain future a fresh lease on life.

Chef Louis Szathmary put it best, I think, when he told me how he categorized the thousands of books, periodicals, pamphlets, broadsides, and ephemeral items on culinary history and food preparation that he had stored in thirty-four rooms of a building he owned on the North Side of Chicago. "When you bet on the horse race, you bet for win, for place, for show," he said. "When you buy books, you buy some to read, some to own, and some for reference. You want to possess the books, you want to own them, you want to hold them. Perhaps you even hope that you will read them. But I will say that most of the books I have ever had, I know what is inside."

I have learned mightily from what the legendary bookman Lawrence Clark Powell called "the trinity of book collector, bookseller, and librarian," the very people I wrote about in *A Gentle Madness* and *Patience & Fortitude,* plus the many others I have met since then and whose insights also have been incorporated in these pages. I especially like the attitude of Louis Daniel Brodsky, the driven collector of all things relating to William Faulkner, a man for whom books were not nearly enough, just a good start. Brodsky began his hunt in the 1960s by reading a great biography of his hero, a life of the author written by Joseph Blotner, and then using it as a "road map" to find people close to Faulkner who might have unique items they would be willing to sell. "Let me tell you another trick about collecting," Brodsky told me at one point in our discussions, explaining why he had chosen *not* to buy a major Faulkner collection assembled by a rival but to continue instead along his own way. "You size up what's there and you decide, I'm either going to go for it or I'm not, because I'm either in this for the long haul, or I'm not, but you have to live by your decisions, and there's no looking back. You have to develop a sense of balance so that if you blow it on one, it'll wash out the next time around."

As we embark forthwith on the pleasant task of sharing sea stories with the gently mad, I am reminded of a volume of literary criticism that I keep on a shelf near my computer, not so much to peruse—and let the record show, I dutifully *did* read it when it came across my desk as a review copy in 1979—but to glance, during idle moments, at the wonderful title the writer Marvin Mudrick chose for his essays, a string of eight words and a question mark that express a sentiment I confess that I savor on a daily basis: *Books Are Not Life but Then What Is?*

CHAPTER 2

A LITTLE HELP
FROM YOUR FRIENDS

There are cynics among us who would have you believe that people become book collectors the day they buy a book they know with some degree of certainty that they will never read—a pithy little wisecrack that has some kernel of truth to it, but one that is not without its flaws. There's another quip just as contemptuous, a translation from the German to the effect that the bibliophile is a person who opens a volume only while wearing white gloves, and even then to read just the back page, a reference to the time when information containing details of publication were printed in a concluding notation known as the colophon. Dismissive or not, either of these characterizations is preferable to the sneer offered up by the poet A. E. Housman: "Bibliophiles: an idiotic class."

In my case, books have always been an important part of my life, and I have always taken pleasure in having many nearby, even if a good number of them go for years without being penetrated beyond the preface. The truth is that I was hoarding books long before I had acknowledged that I had become an antiquarian, although it must be said that I have always acquired materials with the expectation that they would be read or used for reference, if not now, then at some point in the future. For many years I even followed what I called my twenty-year rule, a loosely applied dictum that books—and we are not talking rarities here, just books of the secondhand variety that unfailingly capture my fancy whenever I encounter them—would enjoy my hospitality for at least two decades if there was the slightest hope that I might find some use for them during that period.

As a professional writer with eclectic interests, I maintain a formidable array of research materials that serve my purposes in multiple ways, so a book does not have to be "read through" from beginning to end to justify its keep. If this sounds like heresy, I need only quote Winston Churchill, the eloquent world statesman and Nobel Prize–winning author of many diverting works, who maintained that books—and his shelves are said to have been stocked with up to fifty thousand titles—should be arranged "on your own plan, so that if you do not know what is in them, you at least know where they are. If they cannot be your friends, let them at any rate be your acquaintances." My own feeling in this regard is that I have a pretty good idea of what is *in* the books I have, and what matters most of all is that I am able to lay my hands on what I need when I need it. Having said that, the larger truth is that there is still only so much space available; my garage and cellar are already full to bursting, a bathroom closet that is supposed to store domestic items such as detergents, towels, and the like shelter my beloved pop-up books and my wife's gardening books, and a good-sized storage shed I rent a few miles from my house is rapidly approaching capacity. So much as I might like to keep everything, it is impossible, which is why I try to impose some standards, and for a while the twenty-year rule seemed as good as any course to take.

But as I approach the autumn of my years, as Frank Sinatra was wont to say, I find that twenty years fly by pretty quickly, and some unread books that I bought in the 1970s, though prime candidates for deaccessioning now under my benign policy, have been granted extensions, in some cases outright commutations. One of the great jokes around my household is the Sunday afternoon we set aside every six months or so for "weeding," a rather feeble attempt to find some books that I am willing to give to the Friends of the Goddard Library at Clark University for their semiannual sales, or other organizations that might have some use for them. I usually fill a half dozen boxes or so to donate, but it is never easy, and there have been times when I have shown up first in line to buy back titles that I decided in a fit of breathless anxiety I still had to have after all.

A recent case in point is a book by Ben H. Bagdikian called *The Information Machines,* which I bought in 1971 when it was new, and which stayed on my shelves year after year, scowling at me every time I spotted its bright red, yellow, and orange dust jacket peeking out from the corner slot it had occupied in my basement office. As new technologies arrived on the scene, making the content of Bagdikian's inventory hopelessly out-of-date, I actually thought, albeit briefly, about putting what was then this amusing anachronism in the discard box. But then I started work on *Life Beyond Life,* the third volume in a continuing examination of the general concept of book culture, one in which the shape of "information machines" to come is of immediate concern, and I found that this work, with its now-quotable predictions of the late 1960s, to be an essential source for my work after all.

Less uncertain was my decision to part with *Belgium*—a bulky, two-volume memoir written by Brand Whitlock, the American minister to that country during World War I— which I found at the old Salvation Army bookshop near the Capitol in Washington, D.C., in 1966, while doing research for my master's thesis at the Library of Congress, and which I acquired for one dollar and fifty cents a volume. Published in 1919, this copy had never been read—the pages were still uncut—and probably came out of some bureaucrat's study after a change in administrations, or in the aftermath of a retirement, who knows. I had never come close to reading through all fifteen hundred pages. The truth is that it was pretty slow going, but I held on to it all the same, deciding finally in 1997 that the work might find a more accommodating home elsewhere. A few weeks after leaving the two volumes off in a cardboard box at the Goddard Library, I learned of a heinous instance of a great library being leveled by the German army at the University of Louvain in 1914, weeks after the outbreak of hostilities in Europe—the willful destruction of books is one of the subjects I am addressing in *Life Beyond Life.* I thought immediately about Whitlock's memoirs, assuming, correctly as it turned out, that it would contain some useful discussion of the atrocity. Thankfully for me, *Belgium* did not prove to be a hot item at the Clark sale—somebody at the Friends had penciled in what looked like sixteen dollars for the pair, not the six dollars that seemed more appropriate—and I was able to arrange a worthwhile swap, getting back the volumes I had decided I still needed after all. I could go on and on with similar examples, but the point is that these kinds of book crises happen to me all the time (for another telling example, see the prologue to *Patience & Fortitude* and an account of my desperate attempt to locate a copy of the 1914 edition of the Samuel Pepys library catalog). I have learned, with experience, to err on the side of caution.

The driving force in all this is space, since I would keep everything forever if I could. The home in Milan of the novelist and scholar Umberto Eco is crammed with thirty thousand volumes, many tons of books to be sure, but thirty thousand it is, and thirty thousand it remains, with a zero population growth policy supposedly in force, although some of the discards come to rest variously in an apartment the professor maintains in Bologna where he teaches, a summer home he and his wife have in the Apennines, or their flat in Paris. It was Eco who told me, incidentally, that there are times when "the forgotten book is the most important book you can have." He was referring to an unsightly copy of Aristotle's *Poetics* he had put away years earlier in some remote cubbyhole, only to run across it several years after his wonderful novel of a medieval bookman, *The Name of the Rose*, had achieved international acclaim. A quick examination of the long-neglected volume revealed that it bore striking physical similarities to the book that is at the core of his novel— an ugly copy of Aristotle that is laden with poison. "I had it here all the time," he said, tapping his forehead, noting a larger alchemy at work with many of the books he has in his possession but also has not read. "At first glance, it is inexplicable," he said, that a person is able to pick up a certain volume and realize instantly "that you know everything about the book you need to know." The "phenomenon" at work—and he used that word—is that by constantly picking up and moving books around, an intellectually alert person is "taking stock" of what is inside, "and in the meantime you have read other books that are addressing the same subject; then you realize that you know the book without actually having read it."

I must say that I feel much the same way about the huge accumulation of books in my house. The only volumes that I have shelved in any precise way are my collectibles; the others follow a makeshift kind of order that makes sense to me, either by category—two double-shelved bookcases, for instance, devoted entirely to biographies of authors—or by subject, such as the Dead Sea Scrolls, library history, aviation, naval history, cartography, photography, American artists, the book arts, auction catalogs—a whole panoply of interests. In fiction and poetry, I keep my authors together, but otherwise the layout, seemingly haphazard to strangers, follows a certain logic that works just fine for me. Because the placement has a way of changing from time to time according to the exigencies of the moment and the new connections I find myself making between various works, I am constantly moving things around, from this shelf to that shelf, this room to that one, upstairs to downstairs, poking through each volume with every relocation, registering nuggets of information in the process. Though some might find such a method of absorption a little too "seat of the pants" for their taste, I was pleased to note a similar kind of organization at work at the delightfully cluttered Serendipity Book Store in Berkeley, California, where the widely respected founder and owner, Peter B. Howard, pointedly told me that he is "extremely mistrustful of bookstores that are neat as a pin," and where, in fact, a brilliant patron of many years standing, Ian Jackson, was emboldened to write a learned guide on "the key" to locating books at Serendipity.

About half of the books in my possession are secondhand, and have been acquired from used books stores, flea markets, antiquarian dealers, thrift shops, and library sales. The others are books that I have acquired new or as remainders, either through direct purchase, or as review copies sent to me courtesy of the major American publishing houses. This latter option came into play in 1978 when I was appointed literary editor of the *Worcester Sunday Telegram* and given the task of overseeing a weekly section of reviews, a package that ranged anywhere from six to twelve pieces every week, a task I delighted in through 1991, assuming a responsibility maintained at the newspaper for seventeen years prior to my tenure by Ivan Sandrof, the founder and first president of the National Book Critics Circle, and for whom the organization has named a major award. I already owned hundreds of books when I took the position, but all of a sudden, with what I have gone on record as calling my "dream job," I had access to virtually every new book that was being published in the United States, and the shelves in my home quickly began to sag under the weight of this exhilarating windfall. There was the matter of assigning books to reviewers, of course, but that was just a minor distraction, as publishers were all too willing to send me additional copies of any title that I cared to request for my own use. I was never shy about asking for what I wanted, arguing—quite sensibly, I think—that a literary editor needs to be reading a good number of the books that he is giving others to read, if only to have a critical sense of what is being produced for his pages and to assess the continuing performance of his reviewers. From the very beginning of my tenure I was interviewing authors for a weekly essay I had introduced, a literary feature that I continued to write even after I left the newspaper in 1991 and syndicated in twenty-five newspapers throughout the country, giving it up finally in 1999, after interviewing more than a thousand authors. At the urging of Ivan Sandrof, I always asked the writers I met for a personal inscription in the books that we were discussing. "Don't be shy about this," Ivan made clear to me. "You are going to be spending time with some of the most important writers in the world, and they will be thrilled that you ask them to personalize their books for you."

Well, I wasn't timid about asking for inscriptions at all, and before long I was getting together with every major author that came through Boston, on many occasions traveling to New York for interviews, for a few years going to numerous other places on freelance interview assignments for *Publishers Weekly*. I never turned down an offer from a publicist to meet with someone I viewed as an "important" writer, and there was always the denouement of having each one sign my book. The collection grew rapidly, I daresay indiscriminately in some instances, because along with the certified superstars, there were others I saw whose noble efforts have long since vanished from the literary horizon, though I must say their signed books remain safe with me. But for the writers, artists, and photographers I have supreme admiration for, there came a point where I would bring along much more than the newly released books that we were discussing for my feature articles.

What had happened is that in addition to being a journalist writing about a particular book that had just been published, I wanted to have signed first edition copies of the *other* books these favored authors of mine had previously ushered through the printing press, and it was pretty much at that point—the systematic quest for the earliest copies of selected writers—that I had entered the domain of the bibliophile. Because these books were not readily available in bookstores, I established relationships with a number of antiquarian booksellers, giving them my want lists for authors I felt I might be meeting before long, and for whom I wanted collectible copies of everything they had written for publication in book form. Even though I had a lot to learn about the kinds of things that are collectible, I drew some lines in the sand about the kinds of things that I *didn't* want: such peripheral objects as uncorrected proofs, magazine articles, and signed limited editions of obscure works, rarely significant items whose only reason for being is to create a condition of manufactured rarity. What I wanted was a first edition record of *my* authors as they have been presented to the general readership by trade and university presses. Incidentally, when I say that I don't *collect* uncorrected proofs, I don't, per se, but I do *keep* some of the more interesting ones I receive that come my way for review purposes. This is a fine distinction, I know, but it is relevant. To me, book collecting is synonymous with book hunting, and I do not go *out of my way* to find proofs. Does that mean that if I somehow were to stumble across a bound set of the uncorrected proofs for Robert Stone's great debut work, *A Hall of Mirrors,* winner

in 1967 of the Faulkner Foundation Best First Novel Award—
which as a work-in-progress was called *Children of Light,*
but was changed at the last minute, only to be used nineteen
years later as the title for his fourth novel—I would not consider acquiring it, assuming the price was right, because I
don't collect proofs? Good question; it hasn't happened yet,
so I can't say for sure. But to repeat, what I was interested in
from the beginning—and what I remain interested in now—
is the published work.

Of the hundreds of interviews I conducted over the years,
my experiences with the novelist Joseph Heller are worth
recalling here since they do make an important point as to
the advisability of collecting autographs or inscriptions. I
met Heller for the first time in 1984 at the Ritz-Carlton Hotel
in Boston to talk about his newly released novel, *God
Knows.* When I asked if he would mind signing a couple of
books, he was only too happy to oblige. "Too bad you don't
have a copy of *Catch-22,*" he said before I had a chance to open
up my briefcase. "I understand they're worth a lot of money
these days, especially if you've got one with the dust jacket."
The copy of that very book I thereupon produced for his
approval—fine, in a bright dust jacket, and acquired just the
week earlier from Joe Dermont in Onset, Massachusetts—
brought an appreciative smile to his face. "Maybe you want
me to just *sign* this," he said, demonstrating a keen sense of
the antiquarian market by suggesting delicately that it might
be "worth more if I don't include *your* name," just his. I
replied that the value to me was *personal,* not *monetary,* and
that I would prefer an *inscription,* which means that I
wanted him to write something in addition to his signature.
So he wrote the following on the title page: "To Nick, Who

treasures this first edition, I wish all of the best. (I also wish that I too had a first edition), Joseph Heller, 9/26/84, Boston." It turned out that in the course of going through a recent divorce, Heller's books had been lost somewhere in the domestic shuffle, and he did not possess a first issue copy of his signature work. Twelve years later, when I was interviewed by Brian Lamb on the C-SPAN program *Booknotes*, I told that little story. When Heller and I got together again in 1998 to discuss his memoir, *Now and Then: From Coney Island to Here*, he informed me straightaway that he had enjoyed watching my appearance on television. When it came time for him to inscribe the book, he wrote this: "For Nick Basbanes—To add to his rich collection of Joseph Heller works. And I *still* wish I had a good first edition of *Catch-22*! Joseph Heller, Feb. 25, 1998, Boston."

If I had followed conventional wisdom, as Heller had suggested in our first meeting, then all I would have are two signatures, not this delightful pair of inscriptions. So is *just* the autograph worth more on the open market? Perhaps it is, but you can't prove it by me. As far as I am concerned, a message of some sort is the far more interesting choice, certainly if there is an *association* to be discerned between the author and the recipient, but also for the simple fact that there is more *writing* with the latter. It's all a matter of personal choice, but I would rather have *more* than *less*. My preference, in any case, has always been to have a personal greeting, and I have never regretted it.

While on the subject of signed books, this might be a good time to address the matter of determining authenticity. In the case of my books, I know I have the genuine article because I was there when they were inscribed. I can swear on a stack of sacred texts that the signature of Arthur Miller on my copy of *Death of a Salesman* and the autograph of John Updike on my *Rabbit Run* are the real deal because they wrote their names on the half-title pages as I looked on. But the greatest potential for fraud in the collecting of first editions today is the enhancement of copies by the passing off of books claiming to bear the signatures of authors. How does a person tell if a signature is not a forgery? By knowing *who* you are buying from, for openers, since all reputable dealers guarantee what they sell, and also by asking about the provenance, or prior ownership, of the book in question. A previously unknown copy of Ernest Hemingway's *The Sun Also Rises* that appears on the market, seemingly out of the woodwork, with a marvelous inscription to someone whose relationship with the author is unknown, and if the person selling it, moreover, has no idea where it came from or any paperwork to document the circumstances of how it came to be available, should be treated with great caution. This is especially true with such on-line sources as eBay, where every manner of signed book is being put up for sale by amateurs who have no idea at all of what they are doing, and where it is understood that what is being listed is being sold "as is." I'll have more to say about eBay in chapters 5 and 8.

About a year or so into my book editor's job I became friendly with one of my best freelance reviewers, a brilliant man named Raymond Morin who in his youth had the distinction of finishing first ahead of Leonard Bernstein in a music competition held in Boston. After a brief but distinguished career as a concert pianist, Raymond spent most of his adult life as a highly regarded music critic at a time when our newspaper was still independently owned, and when the management still saw merit in having competent critics on its full-time staff. Though he had retired by the time I took over the position in 1978, Raymond's knowledge of music was extraordinary, and he was a wonderful writer to boot; I immediately began cultivating him as a reviewer for my pages and we quickly became fast friends, forging a friendship that I treasure to this day. It was Raymond, in fact, who suggested that I seek out earlier first editions of important books for my authors to sign, not just the new releases that I was writing about for my weekly features, and it was Raymond who put me in touch with a number of antiquarian booksellers, encouraging me to give them my desiderata. But my most memorable hours with him, I must say, were spent in his home library surrounded by his first editions, feeling, as I liked to say, the "gamma rays" of so much intellectual energy shooting out at me from all four walls of his neatly stacked shelves.

Raymond's books represented a collection begun for the most part as a diversion to pursue in retirement. They were very nice copies, though the truth is they were not outstanding, if only because he was not a stickler on great condition. He had full runs of Henry James and Somerset Maugham in British and American editions, to cite just two of his authors; an admirable accomplishment, but he lacked dust jackets for many of them, and some of the spines had been discolored by extended exposure to sunlight—they were "sunned," according to the jargon—but he was content with what he had. "At my age," he explained, and he was in his mid-seventies at the time, "you seize your opportunities with the realization that you might not have another." But his books had been carefully gathered and deeply appreciated all the same, and I loved them, I do believe, as much as he did, since so many of the authors—Mark Twain, Herman Melville, Nathaniel Hawthorne among them—were favorites of mine as well.

Of overriding significance, from my standpoint, was that I was at the time still an infant in the world of such arcane concepts as issue points, publishing states, foxing, pastedowns, and the like, and there was wisdom to be gleaned from the friendship with Raymond. Before long these terms describing the details that identify a first edition, the successive printings of a book, the condition of oxidation on paper that creates a kind of rust-colored blemish, the sheets glued on the boards of a book, and so many others, would become part of my everyday vocabulary. But much more important than learning the language of collecting was the fact that I had found a mentor, and if there is one piece of advice I have for budding bibliophiles, whatever the object of their desire, it is that they find someone who is not only willing to pass on what they know, but to share with them the enthusiasm that motivated the quest. I remember having coffee with Raymond in his library one night with my wife after a pleasant dinner at a nearby restaurant, and Connie saying to me on the drive home, "You know, we can do that." I knew precisely what she was talking about, of course, and it was right there that I realized—perhaps *accepted* is the more accurate word—that I had crossed the fine line that separates the book lover from the book collector. Raymond, needless to say, was only too happy to share with me some of the things he had learned in his expeditions through the New England countryside, and before long we were making many of these trips together. One day we would drive up to Portsmouth, New Hampshire, for a couple of hours of browsing through the secondhand stores there, then we would swing into Maine for a run by the half dozen or so shops on U.S. Route 1. In the summer we would head down to Cape Cod for a visit to Ralph Titcomb's charming shop on Old King's Highway in East Sandwich, stop in at Ben Muse's cavernous Parnassus book barn in Yarmouth Port, then have some fried clams at Lindsey's in Buzzard's Bay before returning home.

Raymond always carried his tattered copy of Van Allan Bradley's *The Book Collector's Handbook of Values* with him on these trips, an indispensible reference in its day that went through four editions between 1972 and 1982. Following Bradley's death, the task was taken up admirably by Allen and Patricia Ahearn, the owners of Quill & Brush Rare Books in Dickerson, Maryland, and authors of several other excellent books on collecting; their most recent compilation—an encyclopedia, really—*Collected Books: The Guide to Values,* contains information on more than twenty thousand books, with issue points listed for individual titles. This kind of compendium was essential equipment twenty years ago and, even with the Internet search engines of today, is still a basic reference, the only problem being the size—three pounds on my scale—and not the kind of tome you would normally tote around with you at a book fair. I asked Raymond about this habit of his once, why he insisted on carrying along a book he could just as easily consult at home. (Actually, he would leave the book in the car wherever we went and go outside periodically to check a reference or two, using the opportunity to sneak a cigarette at the same time.) Instead of answering me directly, he retrieved a leather-bound octavo from one of his shelves and told me to look at it carefully, and then tell him what I thought it was that I was holding in my hands. At first glance, nothing startling jumped out. The title—*The Sketch Book of Geoffrey Crayon, Gent., No VI*—rang no bells. I noted the place of publication, New York City, and the year, 1820. "Who is Geoffrey Crayon?" I asked, and as someone whose major in college was English and American literature, I suppose I should have been embarrassed by what I would quickly learn. The truth is that I had no idea of who he may have been—though the resonant name of the printer, listed on both the title and copyright pages as C. S. Van Winkle of New York, should have been a sufficient hint.

As I flipped through the pages, it was apparent that the volume contained Part VI and Part VII of this writer's collected sketches, some of them fiction, others essays; the first to appear, "John Bull," meant nothing to me, neither did "The Pride of the Village," but the lengthy story that began on page 51, "The Legend of Sleepy Hollow," raised the hair on my arms. "I found that at a small fair in Connecticut," Raymond told me. "I asked the dealer to hold it aside for me while I went outside to see if it was listed in Bradley." What he learned from his reference book—and what he then acquired for ten dollars—was a first-issue appearance of what is arguably Washington Irving's best-known piece of writing, a story that ranks in company only with "Rip Van Winkle," which had appeared in Parts I–V of the *Sketch Book,* published in a companion volume in 1819, and also under the pseudonym of Geoffrey Crayon. "I should have known when I saw that the printer was C. S. Van Winkle," I mumbled, but it was a lesson learned on why doing your homework is so necessary. When Raymond died in 1988, his books were sold at a small auction in Sturbridge, Massachusetts, and I was determined to acquire the Geoffrey Crayon, providing, of course, that it was within my budget. I take some satisfaction in the knowledge that none of the dealers who attended the sale showed the slightest bit of interest in the item; they were all focused on Henry James, Somerset Maugham, and H. G. Wells. The name of the pseudonymous author, apparently, meant nothing to them either, and the mimeographed list of lots merely gave titles, no descriptions, which is why I was able to acquire it for twenty dollars. I am still looking for the earlier volume, but my guess is that if it ever comes my way, it will have to be through means that are just as improbable, since the last time the two parts were sold together at auction (in 1995), they went for thirteen thousand dollars.

Coming as it did at a dispersal sale occasioned by the death of a close friend, my acquisition of the *Sketch Book* was bittersweet, to say the least, especially since Raymond and I had attended a number of auctions just like this one together; I even brought my own Bradley along to his sale and left it out in the car in silent tribute, just as he surely would have done. Raymond enjoyed going to these sales not so much to buy but to be among other book people. For me, these auctions—and like book fairs, they can range in sophistication from informal gatherings in rented church halls like this one to the dazzling performances staged at Christie's, Sotheby's, and Swann Galleries—provided yet another learning opportunity, with the added prospect of homing in, wherever possible, on any targets of opportunity that might present themselves. There was one sale in particular we attended together in 1984 to benefit a library-friends group that had an embarrassingly low turnout, undoubtedly because of the fierce winter storm that was predicted for that night, which left eight inches of fresh snow on the ground by the next morning. The weather forecasts were not intimidating enough to keep us away, though, and I had no trouble getting the books I was interested in, most notably a copy of Samuel Johnson's *Lives of the Most Eminent English Poets,* not a first edition by any means, but a gorgeously bound and decorated three-volume set published in 1801 all the same, and a similarly beautiful four-volume set of *The Diary and Correspondence of Samuel Pepys,* a nice example of the fourth impression published in London in 1854. With my cost for these seven volumes totaling something like fifty dollars, I had every reason to feel that I was on a roll. When the auctioneer opened the bidding for a collection of some forty-eight hundred postcards, and when it appeared that nobody was interested in offering so much as fifty dollars for them, I impulsively raised my hand. "Sixty," a woman at the rear of the hall then chimed in, setting in motion an exchange in which the two of us kept upping the ante by ten-dollar increments, back and forth, until we got to two hundred dollars, at which point the advances went up by twenty-five dollars a pop. When we got to two hundred seventy-five dollars, my friend Raymond, who to this point had been oblivious to my activity, having assumed, quite correctly, that this was not an area I had ever demonstrated any interest whatsoever in beforehand, noticed my hand waving in the air. "This is you?" he asked in an incredulous stage whisper. "This is my last bid," I whispered, having decided on the fly that I wouldn't go over three hundred dollars, at which point the woman in the back of the room withdrew from the competition, and eight large boxes of postcards, stacked on a steel dolly at the front of the room, were mine. "You don't collect postcards," Raymond said, shaking his head with amused reproach. "I do now," I told him, a response that I would have an opportunity to reaffirm in a matter of minutes when my erstwhile rival for the lot, an antiques dealer who had come down from Vermont, introduced herself and asked if I would entertain an offer for "the carton with the kings and queens of Europe in it."

Given the fact that this collection had been the pride and joy of Francis Henry Taylor, director successively of the Worcester Art Museum from 1931 to 1940, the Metropolitan Museum of Art in New York from 1940 to 1955, and back again to direct the museum in Worcester from 1955 until his death in 1957 at the age of fifty-four, and that his tenure at these prestigious institutions paralleled their most spectacular years of growth, I became protective and unwilling to see it broken up and sold piecemeal at flea markets, one card at a time, this king for ten dollars, that queen for five dollars, this Venetian *piazzetta* for two dollars, these first-ever views of the tomb of Tutankhamen for whatever the traffic might bear. I also knew beforehand that Taylor had been a discriminating collector of art books. Born and raised in Philadelphia, he was the son of a prominent surgeon who had served as president of the Library Company of Philadelphia, and had passed a love of art and a sense of connoisseurship on to his son. Taylor's private library, in fact, had been acquired from his estate by the same person who after some years of not knowing what to do with the postcards donated them to this particular organization and admitted afterward to me how relieved he was that they had gone to a collector who intended to keep them together. So without knowing a whole lot about Francis Henry Taylor at the time, I still felt a bond with him, a feeling of solidarity with someone whose passion for a gathering of artifacts for his personal amusement was in danger of being scattered to the four winds, and I got it for what amounted to loose change. So my reply to the woman's offer went something like this: "Madam, let me say that I know nothing about the contents of this collection other than the fact that it was put together by a man of formidable intellect and substance, and that I feel obliged to retain it as a unit or, failing that, to at least allow it to change hands in a manner that is commensurate with the dignity that it deserves. Let me also say that if you really wanted the kings and the queens of Europe, you should have hung in there for one more bid, because I was finished at two hundred seventy-five dollars, and you could have had them all." I later calculated that I paid something on the order of a nickel a card for the eight boxes, a trifle in 1984, an even greater trifle now, especially when you factor in the historical background I developed that gives added meaning—a texture, if you will—to this highly distinctive collection, and why I am pleased to report that after eighteen years, I remain its loyal custodian. But that is only part of the story.

Once I had Francis Henry Taylor's postcards, it became necessary for me to know more about Francis Henry Taylor; the *New York Times* had devoted considerable space to his obituary in 1957, and there were hundreds of news clips in the files at the Worcester *Telegram & Gazette* to consult. That was a solid start. I then talked to people in Worcester who knew the man and worked with him, and I sought out copies of the erudite books that Taylor wrote, most notably *The Taste of Angels* (1948), a best-selling history of art-collecting from the time of Ramses to Napoleon. As pure coincidence would have it, right around the time that I bought the postcards, I interviewed the internationally acclaimed portrait photographer Yousuf Karsh, who had just published a collection of his best-known images. On page 59 of the book, titled *Karsh,* appears a full-page portrait of Taylor, in profile, overlooking the grand hall of the Worcester Art Museum, taken just a few months before his death. In the caption, Karsh wrote this: "To think of Francis Henry Taylor is to remember his dark eyes, luminous with intelligence, and that strong Florentine nose. Art was his life, and to the collection, appreciation, and preservation of great works of art he devoted his energy and discrimination."

As Taylor traveled the world acquiring art for the museums he directed, he bought postcards by the dozen, maintaining, so far as I can determine, a kind of visual record of the places he was scouring for new material, all of which he carefully indexed and kept in eight large filing boxes. Of the forty-eight hundred cards in the collection, most date from the early 1900s, many of them are in suites, and all are in perfect condition (the word *mint* truly applies here). There are some marvelous views of monuments, sculptures, interiors, tapestries, bronzes, paintings, buildings—indeed, there is what amounts to an architectural tour of Europe, including views of many landmarks that were destroyed in World War II. Only about four hundred or so were actually postmarked and mailed—those had been sent to Taylor from acquaintances and colleagues traveling abroad—and all are still stored in their original boxes. As my friend Raymond astutely noted, I was not, until that one impulsive instant, a postcard collector, and in the years that have elapsed since I became one on a snowy New England night, I have not acquired any others. When I am ready to part with what I have, they will go to someone, or perhaps some place, with a committed interest in protecting this small but telling footnote in the life of an important figure in the American arts movement. Call it a nod of respect to another collector, whatever, but the truth is that I have great admiration for this man's tenacity, and I am pleased to have been selected by circumstance to keep some memory of it alive.

In addition to the auctions we attended together, Raymond Morin introduced me to book fairs, essential take-in events for the serious book hunter twenty years ago, just as essential today. Many beginners might ask, OK, great, where do you meet people with like-minded interests in this day and age, especially with the Internet providing so much "interactivity" to the book world, but very little in the way of personal contact? My answer is that you should go to the book fairs when they come through your neck of the woods. Book fairs are wonderful because they bring fresh faces and fresh stock from all points of the compass into one hall for a couple of days a year, and you have a chance to make direct contact with them, and to schmooze with others like yourself who are just starting out. I always take a notebook with me to these festivals—the Cleveland, Ohio, collector Robert Jackson calls them quatrocento balls—and nothing amuses me more than to jot down how nicely my own copies of certain books compare with what is being offered today, and to see how sagaciously I bought ten, fifteen, twenty years earlier. You also have an opportunity to learn firsthand exactly what a dealer means when a certain book is deemed to be *fine* or *very good*, and to measure one bookseller against another on matters of variety, condition, description, and pricing.

Not only will you find yourself picking up the jargon, you will get your name entered on mailing lists, you will scoop up as many catalogs and bookseller directories as you can carry, and if you're lucky, you might even come across a book that you've been trying for years to locate at a price you believe to be reasonable. For beginners especially, even if you aren't there to buy, you should be alert to what is going on around you. Look at how people who seem to know what they are doing pick up a book, how they cradle it in one hand while carefully turning pages with the other, how they never lie an open volume flat on a surface and risk snapping its spine. Books are resilient objects, but they are not indestructible, and you will learn by watching how to give them the respect they deserve.

As you establish a rapport with dealers—and that, frankly, comes from buying books from them on a fairly regular basis—they will help you refine your interests and develop your collection. Indeed, some of the really outstanding collections of the past hundred years or so have been due, in no small measure, to the imagination and counsel of an interested bookseller. A good deal of the core collection of Harry Elkins Widener, which was donated to Harvard University after the collector's death in 1912 aboard the *Titanic,* was shaped by Dr. A. S. W. Rosenbach of Philadelphia. The famous collection devoted to "books that made a difference" assembled by the spy novelist Ian Fleming, and the inspiration for the great 1963 exhibition known as "Printing and the Mind of Man," was actually the brainchild of the London dealer Percy H. Muir. There are many instances where a similar accord has taken place, and not only among private collectors, but in academic and research libraries as well.

This should come as no surprise to anyone who pays

attention, because dealers, for the most part, are intelligent people whose true stock in trade is their knowledge, which is why so many of them have specialties, and their integrity, which they build over time by earning your trust and maintaining your confidence. They are also, by and large, friendly and decent people who have learned what they know from others. Every bookseller I have interviewed—be it Pierre Berès in Paris, John Maggs in London, Carlo Chiesa in Milan, Bill Reese in New Haven, Leona Rostenberg and Madeleine Stern in New York, Priscilla Juvelis in Cambridge, or Bernie Rosenthal in Berkeley—has credited, at some point in our conversations, the impact of a mentor in their professional development. What I also have learned is that dealers are only too happy to share some of their trade secrets with serious collectors. I am not suggesting by any means that you ask dealers to conduct a formal seminar for you, rather that you never hesitate to ask questions, and that you give credence to what you hear.

Just as important as asking questions is reading their catalogs, since so much of their expertise is crystallized in the descriptions they write of the books they are offering for sale. As the New York bookseller Fred Schreiber made clear in his interview with me, the raison d'être of a bookseller's catalog is to state in the clearest of terms *why* a particular book, especially an obscure title that most people have never heard of before, is an essential acquisition. Schreiber explained the challenge every bookseller faces when writing a formal description for a catalog: "What is this book about? What is there about it that justifies the price I have determined it should command?" Every statement a bookseller makes about the book must be true, Schreiber stressed, and "every claim must be supported by evidence." Resourceful dealers will encourage you to give them your want lists, and a good idea is to give them a sense of how much money you are willing to spend. They will learn pretty quickly what your budget limitations are; if you are a steady customer, you will get advance notice that a coveted item has been located and is available for your perusal prior to either being entered in a catalog, listed on a website, or offered to someone else.

Book fairs run the gamut in size, from modest gatherings of thirty or forty dealers in remote regions of the country who hold court on a Saturday or a Sunday, to larger, more elaborate undertakings that often feature more than two hundred of the most prominent booksellers from all over North America and Europe, and which run for several days, beginning on a Thursday or Friday night, and continuing through the weekend. The first session is by far the most important one to attend, and it behooves you to be there at the opening bell, since the best material has a way of disappearing fast. An admission fee is charged at most fairs, ranging in price from two dollars for the Albuquerque, New Mexico, Antiquarian Book Fair to thirty-five dollars for every session of the New York International Book Fair, including the all-important "preview" on opening night. One of the most prestigious book fairs anywhere is held every November in Boston in the Hynes Memorial Auditorium on Boylston Street next to the Boston Public Library. Uncommonly appealing about this fair is the fact that *another* fair offering the stock of a whole other set of dealers one rung down in stature from the Antiquarian Booksellers Association of America (ABAA) contingent is held on the same dates, in a large indoor parking lot across the street from the auditorium. Known, in fact, as the Boston Book, Print & Ephemera Show at the Garage, the competing fair is organized by veteran trade show organizer Bernice Bornstein, and is well attended by everyone, including the dealers from the "main event" next door; indeed, the ABAA dealers admit to being some of the most enthusiastic customers in the garage, where a number of the exhibitors sell their wares off the tailgates of their station wagons, creating a festive atmosphere that is unique among book fairs in the United States.

Once you have established a rapport with a bookseller, particularly one who will be exhibiting at a fair you plan to attend, you are wise to ask about getting a complimentary pass, since every participant has a certain number of freebies to spread around among favored customers. With the demise in 1999 of the trade magazine *AB Bookman's Weekly,* which maintained a listing of scheduled events, the most reliable calendars of forthcoming fairs are now announced on the web. I have found the most useful site for this information to be www.bookfairs.com. Another site equally as helpful is www.booksalefinder.com, a state-by-state listing of all forthcoming library discard and donation sales in the United States, an attraction for bibliophiles of another sort altogether, but not-to-be-missed events all the same; ignore these at your peril.

As you go to more and more of these book events, and as you meet more and more dealers, you undoubtedly will want to start spending some time in secondhand bookstores and antiquarian shops. The ABAA publishes an excellent directory of its members, available free of charge at all fairs or by contacting the organization through its website, www.abaa.org. Every regional organization of booksellers has its own directory, all of them broken down by geographic section, and easily found through the various search engines. For links to dealers outside of the United States, a good place to start looking is www.ilab-lila.com, site of the International League of Antiquarian Booksellers, and www.worldbookdealers.com, the new kid on the block, with some exceptionally informative features available as well.

If you haven't already guessed it by now, *booking* is a big deal for me. Whenever I go into a new city, be it for purposes of conducting an interview, giving a talk, or doing research in a library, the first thing I do after making sure the plumbing works in my hotel room is to scout out the bookstores in town. For new books, I have to confess a special affection for the independents, a proud breed that deserves the unbending support of readers everywhere. My particular passion, I must also say, is secondhand books, the antiquarian material to be sure, but secondhand stores have a special place in my heart, not least because they are an endangered species, especially in the big cities where rents are high. A few of the huge emporiums steadfastly remain, the most notable among them being the Strand in New York City, Powell's in Portland, Oregon, Powell's in Chicago, Second Story in Washington, D.C., and suburban Maryland, the Brattle Book Store in Boston, Serendipity in Berkeley, California, John K. King Used and Rare Books in Detroit, Book Baron in Anaheim, California, and Wonder Book in Frederick, Maryland.

"We succeed primarily because of our ability to buy large diversified libraries, which offer an alternative to what the new bookstores in the D.C. area offer," Allan J. Stypeck, owner of Second Story Books, told me. "In Washington, the average book buyer has a college degree and considers books a necessary part of daily life. The income level is substantially higher too since Washington, where the government creates a recession-proof shield, protects us from the ebb and flow of the economy." Stypeck agreed that the Internet has taken its toll on some of the other larger secondhand stores. "Shorey's in Seattle is a perfect example," he said. "They were a huge store, and by all accounts doing a decent business, but they closed their retail outlet anyway in 2000, and went full steam ahead with the on-line end of the business."

For all the attention a transition like this one makes—and Shorey's was a West Coast institution, in business since 1890—it is the middle-level place of business that is under assault by the Internet these days, though like the Energizer Bunny, some eight thousand of them keep on going and going; there are, in fact, some terrific references available, *The Used Book Lover's Guides* by David S. and Susan Siegel, that identify a good many of them in seven regions across North America, and offer information on hours of operation, directions, and nature of available stock. Detailed information on what these sturdy paperbacks contain, and how to obtain them, is available at www.bookhunterpress.com. Another innovation that holds great promise for the health and well-being of the open shop is the cooperative store, where a number of small dealers rent shelf space in one building at a nominal fee and authorize a single person—usually the principal tenant of the building—to sell their books. One of the most successful operations along these lines, I am pleased to say, is the Worcester Antiquarian Book Center directly across Salem Street in Worcester, Massachusetts, from the city's new public library. The main tenant is Donald V. Reid, owner of the delightfully eclectic Ben Franklin Bookstore, who rents shelf space to a dozen other dealers from around the region, and acts as agent on their behalf.

On the matter of following a certain protocol with booksellers, there are a few suggestions to bear in mind. It is not a good idea, for instance, to haggle with a dealer you have never done business with before, although if it is your custom to pay for what you buy in cash, you might do well to make that preference known while discussing the purchase. Such a circumstance just might make a difference in the final price, since many dealers would prefer not having to give a percentage of their earnings to a credit card company, and let's face it, everyone gets a good feeling out of having crisp bills to tuck into their wallet. It is in no way bad form to mention any flaws you might notice in your scrutiny of a volume that have not been stated in the dealer's description. If a binding is loose and has not been noted, or if you determine in your examination of an illustrated book that some of the plates are missing, or if you suspect that repairs have been made to the binding that are not identified, then by all means you should inquire whether this might justify another price quotation. If you are buying more than one book from a dealer, you could gently ask—just ask, that's all, especially if there is the promise of more business down the line—"Is that the best you can do for the lot?" This is not to say that looking for an adjustment on a listed price is unheard-of in the rare book business, but it is not nearly as much a part of the culture as it is among antiques dealers, where haggling is considered de rigueur. Booksellers for the most part take great pride in the research they do on the stock they offer for sale, and if they are going to be successful, they are not going to get very far by charging more for the same books than the competition, especially in this day and age with so many on-line resources available to make comparisons. If you are a gambler, and if you are willing to roll the dice on waiting to see if a book you want is still available at the end of a fair, then you might saunter by the booth on the final day, in the final hour, and quietly wonder if something might be done in your behalf, especially if the traffic has been slow, and if the clock is ticking down to last call. Given a choice, most dealers would much prefer driving a station wagon back home that is empty to one that has been reloaded with unsold inventory, but that approach is fraught with risk, the most obvious being that the item you are counting on has already been sold to somebody else. Minor Myers, the collector of "everything and anything from the eighteenth century," told me that he has two "book shopping rules" that he applies, not just at fairs, but everywhere. "Rule Number One is that you buy the book because it is one that you have wanted for some time, and is on your list of things that you are really looking for, and you just may never see it again. A Rule Two purchase is more whimsical, and involves books that happen to strike your fancy. You buy these books because you know intuitively that if you don't buy them now, you will regret for years not having bought them when you had the chance." This is not much different from the Sanford Berger should've rule I discussed in chapter 1, and yet another variation on my own bite-the-bullet rule.

Something else my friend Raymond impressed upon me early on was the advisability of keeping a catalog of my collection, one that contained not only the basic bibliographical data of the books I was gathering, but details that documented where, when, and from whom they were acquired, and how much was paid. When I got my first computer in 1982—an Eagle II that now, like so many other obsolete machines from that embryonic period, is an example of "dead media"—one of the first tasks I did was to create a computerized listing of my books that incorporated pretty much the same details Raymond had categorized in his loose-leaf notebook, only I had a search engine to help me keep track of my core holdings. The software I used then is pretty antiquated by today's standards, and I have long since migrated my information over to a professional database. I strongly urge anyone who is assembling a collection of any sophistication to follow this advice. For my purposes, a basic FileMaker Pro software package has worked out just fine; mine is the 3.3 series, which is more than adequate to my needs, but I temper that with the declaration that I still do all my writing on WordPerfect 5.1, preferring that discontinued software over everything else that has come down the line in the decade since its introduction, including Microsoft Word in all its various mutations.

By keeping track of the books you buy, you also are making it easier on yourself when it comes time to bid your beloved treasures farewell, either by private sale to a dealer or another collector, consigned for auction, given to a loved one, or donated as a charitable gift to an institution. Like any other valuable commodity, how much was paid for an item and how much it is worth on the open market now are factors that will have to be calculated, and the only way to do this properly is by maintaining accurate records. These issues are of such concern that they were the subject of a well-attended forum mounted early in 2001 by the Center for the Book at the Library of Congress, the principal issue on the agenda being how libraries and collectors can facilitate donations in a manner that benefits recipients and benefactors alike. Though certainly not for everyone, giving is an option that some collectors should bear in mind when the time comes for them to decide the disposition of their cherished books and assorted knickknacks. When people begin to wonder what their collections are "worth," they are well advised to have their holdings professionally appraised, and a fair market value established. This is mandatory, in fact, if tax deductions are going to be part of the calculus. If the materials are of sufficient value, the collectors may just want to weigh the benefits of donating them to an institution that has demonstrated an unequivocal interest in what they have gathered so lovingly over so many years. In the case of educational institutions, it is not a bad idea to be reassured that the material supports the academic curriculum, and will not get lost in a dusty storage cellar somewhere or suffer a fate that is even worse than that: be sold quietly on the open market by the institution for cold cash. Some collectors have worked out arrangements whereby they sell part of their library for cash and give the rest to an institution as a fully deductible gift—the transfer of the Michael Zinman Collection of Early American Imprints to the Library Company of Philadelphia in 2000 is the most notable example of recent years. These options are particularly attractive to people who had the good fortune of buying material twenty or thirty years ago when prices were low, and are faced with serious capital gains issues if they opt to sell now at a considerable margin of profit. Whatever option is chosen, the process is made simpler by the keeping of careful records.

What has been especially useful to me in my electronic catalog is what I call my "comment" field, a little chat box that allows me to say what I think is notable about the books I treasure most dearly, including little peripheral tidbits I have picked up in my research, explaining, in many cases, the reasons that persuaded me to acquire the items in the first place. These miscellaneous notations are often subjective and spontaneous comments, best recorded at once, in the glowing aftermath of consummation; otherwise they are certain to be lost forever. If a book wins a Pulitzer Prize or a National Book Award, if it is a novel that was the basis of a film produced under another name, I will enter that as well—anything that adds texture to the item, gives it a little history, provides some pizzazz. Unlike other collectors who want nothing but pristine copies, I like books that bear evidence of prior ownership, a nice bookplate, a presentation inscription to a child at Christmas, an insightful annotation by a careful reader from two or three generations past. If there are any distinguishing bibliographical details about the book—the issue points we talk about time and time and time again, this is the place to enter them.

I like knowing, for instance, that my copy of Wilmarth Sheldon Lewis's 1957 Sandars Lecture published by Cambridge University Press bears this inscription on the front pastedown: "To Lewis and Juliette from Lefty." There is no date, no place, or any other information included, just "Lefty," which is probably why the dealer on Martha's Vineyard to whom my wife paid five dollars for the book had no reason to know that "Lefty" was the nickname of the author, whose great specialty—the Horace Walpole Library he gathered and gave to Yale University, along with his fabulous house in Farmington, Connecticut—was the subject of the lecture. The question that follows, of course, is whether or not this little detail makes the book *worth* much more than what Connie paid for it. My sense is that it does, but the next question of course is, to whom? However many Lefty Lewis collectors there may be out there is a matter of small specu- lation, so I am not suggesting that this item is worth much more than forty or fifty dollars, but that is not my concern here. What matters is that I have discerned something that is pertinent to this copy of an important bibliographical text, and when my collection of books about books makes its way to other shelves, either premortem or postmortem is beside the point, there is a little gloss here that has become a part of the record, and that effort, it seems to me, is something that is worth doing. That is part of what makes the exercise so consuming, so worthwhile, and is yet another example of how I have benefited from getting a little help from my friends.

CHAPTER 3

GOING WITH THE FLOW

Four weeks after the terrorist attack on New York City had toppled the World Trade Center towers in Lower Manhattan, a library of 446 monuments of Western literature went on the auction block at Christie's Galleries in Rockefeller Plaza, just two miles uptown from the still-smoldering rubble of what by then was already being called Ground Zero. Coupled as it was with an alarming downturn in the American economy, which had been growing increasingly evident in the days leading up to the devastation, the timing of the Abel E. Berland sale on October 8 and 9, 2001, prompted some observers to confide dismal expectations; a few had even urged a postponement, arguing that the last thing a grieving public would be interested in at such a tentative period was rare books. But then there were people in positions of leadership, the president of the United States foremost among them, exhorting their countrymen to resume a normal life, an appeal, in this instance, that ultimately carried the day.

Still, to say there were no misgivings among the organizers of the Berland sale would be misleading, yet when the final results were tabulated, a number of truisms had been reaffirmed. Not surprisingly, the most obvious involved the most spectacular purchases, several of which established records for books sold at auction, proving yet again that objects of unquestioned significance will always command the attention of connoisseurs. A comment offered four months later by an auction house specialist on the positive results of American furniture sales at both Christie's and Sotheby's in the face of the continuing recession applied with equal pertinence to the Berland sale. "The market was rock solid and did not go down," John B. A. Nye told the *New York Times*. "It's a thoughtful marketplace, where collectors, not investors, are doing the buying."

Just as telling, though not nearly as dramatic, was the interest shown in lots offered on the second day of the Berland sale. These were titles that for the most part could be described as books that discriminating people very much *wanted* to have and would be delighted to own, but in many instances decided they didn't necessarily *need* to have, given the obvious uncertainties of world affairs at the time. Most of these lots did sell within their range of estimates, to be sure, though forty-nine did not sell at all, clearly the result of a "reality check" that had taken hold among the professionals in the gallery who were tendering the bids. The sale was divided into two sections, with the marquee material going on the block in prime time on a Monday evening, and the second-tier materials following in a session that began at ten o'clock the following morning. Aptly, the differences between the two were like night and day. A few salient examples from each session are instructive.

For an immaculate copy of the 1623 edition of William Shakespeare's dramatic works, commonly known as the First Folio, an anonymous telephone bidder outdueled the Los Angeles bookseller Lou Weinstein of Heritage Books in a dramatic showdown that became the centerpiece of a television broadcast aired on the cable network C-SPAN, claiming the prize with a final bid of $5.6 million. Once Christie's had added on a commission, known as the buyer's premium, the price had soared to $6.16 million, and that did not include the additional levy of sales taxes. The presale estimate for this volume, in remarkably fine condition and bearing the prior ownership signature of the poet John Dryden, was $2 to $3 million, demonstrating yet again the wisdom of the late jazz pianist Fats Waller, whose enduring phrase, "One never knows, do one?" seemed uncommonly appropriate here. Results for some other notable high spots sold in the auction—and make no mistake, this was very much a high spot sale—included $941,000 for a pristine copy of William Blake's *Songs of Innocence* (1789), $358,000 for a first edition copy of Sir Isaac Newton's *Principia Mathematica* (1687), and $226,000 for the Holford-Rosenbach copy of Izaak Walton's *The Compleat Angler, or the Contemplative Man's Recreation* (1653).

After the first session had concluded, Lou Weinstein was asked by C-SPAN journalist Richard Hall why he had bid so much for the First Folio, why he had, in fact, forced his unknown opponent on the telephone to pay more than twice the anticipated price before he himself withdrew from the competition. "I had a customer who wanted this copy very badly," Weinstein said, adding that he already had another copy of the same book in stock, "but I had advised him to wait and go after this one." What Weinstein was voicing, in a most elemental way, was the continuing relevance of a tenet articulated decades earlier by the late bookseller John F. Fleming, that just three factors come into play when assessing the monetary value of a *great* book: "condition, condition, condition."

Outside of the obvious sentiment expressed, the key word in that description—and it is the reason I have underscored it—is *great,* especially when it is used to evaluate different copies of the same title. What Weinstein was saying, in essence, was that his client was willing to pay almost $6 million for a *superior* copy of a book he could have had in lesser condition and at a fraction of the price. Unlike so many other surviving Shakespeare folios of 1623—and there are about 250 of them in the world—all *leaves,* or sheets, were present in this copy, the margins remained untrimmed, and the seventeenth-century binding was contemporary to the time of publication. There was also the provenance, or documented prior ownership—the lineage, in essence, in this case the great English poet John Dryden—that elevated the level of its desirability to even loftier heights.

A few hours before the bidding began, I was asked by Richard Hall to explain for the C-SPAN audience why I thought someone would pay upward of $1 million for a "little book" like Blake's *Songs of Innocence,* or several times that amount for a First Folio of Shakespeare. "It's just paper," after all, was the unstated implication, and the text, in both instances, is readily available, free of charge, to anyone with a library card or the ability to drive a search engine on a computer. As we spoke for the cameras, the two books in question were lying open in front of me on a table, the "little" Blake (as if size had anything to do with the value one way or the other) with its twenty-one relief and white-line etchings printed in green and hand-colored by the artist, one of only two copies privately owned, and the Shakespeare, opened at the famous engraving of the playwright by Martin Droeshout that faces the title page.

As I pondered how best to answer the question, I ran my hand lightly over each book and offered the opinion that this was the closest I would ever come, in an artifactual way, to having direct contact with either of these writers as human beings, to being able to feel, if only in a visceral sense, the bursts of energy that had flowed from their creative spirits onto paper. In the instance of the *Songs of Innocence,* my fingers ran across pages handled and decorated by the artist himself—"his fingerprints are here," I exclaimed with a mild flourish—since Blake executed every step of the bookmaking process himself, the artwork, the poetry, the illuminations, the stitching on the binding. As for the Shakespeare, I noted that in lieu of any known manuscript material—and nothing of artistic consequence in the playwright's hand has come down through the generations to our time—much of what we have of his work derives from this printed book, conceived and seen through the press by two fellow actors, John Heminge and Henry Condell, seven years after his death. "If you accept the premise that these, then, are iconic objects," I reasoned, "and if you accept that in the case of Shakespeare, this is the most important book ever printed in the English language, then you can begin to understand how it is that someone with the means to buy such a book would not hesitate to spend whatever it takes to acquire it, and have the extraordinary privilege of being able to commune with it on a daily basis."

When it finally came time to sell the Shakespeare later that night, at least two people—the anonymous victor, and the client represented by the underbidder, Lou Weinstein—were willing to spend more than $6 million for a prize that only one of them could have, and at one point in the action the advances were being made in $200,000 increments. As frenetic as such a pitched battle may appear to the casual observer, it is that elegantly straightforward reality—an all-out contest conducted on common ground—that constitutes the true beauty of an auction, since open competition is the most reliable way to establish the market value of any object at any particular time. Similar dynamics were in play for the other remarkable treasures put up for sale by the retired real estate developer from Chicago who had decided it was time to allow a new generation of collectors the same pleasure of ownership that he had enjoyed for so many years, with some of his books representing once-in-a-lifetime opportunities.

As for the second-tier items from Berland's library that were put on the block—books that were very nice, to be sure, but that were by no means impossible to find elsewhere—the results highlighted two other truisms about the collecting world. Phrased simply, they go like this: To get books they feel they *have* to have, there are people who will move heaven and earth, regardless of what is going on in the world; books they would *like* to have, on the other hand, but do not feel they *need* to have, can always wait for another day, especially during difficult times. The larger point to be made from all this is that there are limits to how far even the most motivated collectors are willing to go, and figures posted at the

Berland auction, which will be remembered in bibliophilic circles as the first major book sale of the twenty-first century, bear out both of these points quite tellingly. While it is true that the $14.4 million spent topped by $2 million the presale estimate, there had been quiet hope expressed that the prices would be much higher. Were it not for the fact that more than $6 million, or 40 percent of the total spent, had gone to cover the purchase of a singularly outstanding book, the sale might even have been judged a disappointment, if not an outright disaster. Indeed, 49 lots, or 11 percent of the 446 offered, were bought in by the house, meaning that they failed to meet the reserve, or minimum acceptable amount placed on them, and failed to sell.

The first session of the sale, held on a Monday night, was set aside for 120 high spots, and the gallery responded enthusiastically by spending $12 million; starting at 10 A.M. the next day, the remaining 326 lots went on the block and concluded later that afternoon, garnering a little more than $2 million. "Everything considered, it wasn't bad at all," Francis Whalgren, head of the rare books department for the auction house, said of Part II, though it certainly was not the robust result that he and his colleagues had been hoping for, but they were satisfied all the same, relieved even, given the fact that in order to win the consignment away from archrival Sotheby's earlier in the year, they had put up an advance rumored to be $10 million. If the sale had fallen below that figure, the auction house would have kept the books that did not sell for future disposition, but Abel Berland was guaranteed a minimum return of that amount regardless of what happened in the gallery, and regardless, for that matter, of what happened on the morning of September 11.

In addition to the First Folio, there also were Second

(1632), Third (1663), and Fourth (1685) Folios of Shakespeare, and they realized heady sums as well. It is worth noting that when Abel Berland acquired the Shakespeare folios in 1970, they replaced copies of the same books already in his collection, raising the valid question, why in the world would he spend serious money—and, in fact, spend years badgering the bookseller John Fleming to part with them from his personal collection—for items that were already represented in his own library? The answer: "I always made it a point to move up in quality whenever I could," Berland had told me. Simply put, he wanted better copies. In a similar context, the late collector of twentieth-century American fiction, Carter Burden, once spent $19,250 at a Swann Galleries auction in 1992 for an exceedingly scarce copy of *Hike and the Aeroplane* (1912), a book he already had in his massive collection; only the replacement copy of the first book written by the Nobel Laureate Sinclair Lewis under the pseudonym Tom Graham had a dust jacket—Burden's original copy did not. Though Burden did a good deal of negotiating on his own, he relied heavily on the advice of four prominent dealers, Peter B. Howard of Berkeley, California, Ralph B. Sipper of Santa Barbara, California, Glenn Horowitz of New York City, and the bookseller who introduced him to each of these professionals when he was a neophyte testing the waters, the late Marguerite A. "Margie" Cohn, owner for many years of House of Books in New York.

To make absolutely certain he always got the best copies possible, Berland told me that he also relied on the expert judgment of established booksellers, in the instance of the Shakespeare folios, the late John Fleming. "I want to deal with someone who is responsible," he maintained. "I want the books to be collated. I want to be able to return the book if it is not right, and what you pay for that service is worth every penny." The only time Berland admitted to not using the services of a dealer, he wound up bidding against himself at a Christie's auction for a book he dearly wanted, not knowing that the bookseller, who he could not locate after desperately trying to find him, had shown up at the last minute to bid on his behalf. The California collector Lloyd N. Cotsen, creator of a massive library of children's books now installed at Princeton University, offered the same sentiment in different words. Intent on gathering as many important books as he could in the least amount of time—he was on a mission in the late 1980s and early 1990s to create as a memorial to his late wife and son a "living library" that now numbers eighty thousand volumes—Cotsen bought huge runs of material that had been assembled by others with great care and keen insights. "I didn't have time to put the collection together one book at a time, so I looked for entire collections," he told me. "When I buy a whole collection, I am buying the intelligence that went into creating it. That is worth something, and I am happy to pay that premium."

On the advisability of buying up, or acquiring better copies of books to replace examples of lesser quality of the same titles, the principle applies at every level of collecting. As one simple example, I cite my own purchase fifteen years or so ago of a decent copy of *The Natural* (1952), Bernard Malamud's wonderful first novel, the basis of a fine Robert Redford film, and arguably the best work of fiction ever written about baseball. I have always been a great fan of Malamud's, and cite him among the handful of American authors I dearly wish I had been privileged to interview for my literary column, but was never able to arrange. Still, I made it a point to seek out first edition copies of his works, and I had succeeded in every instance except for his first published book, which is not surprising, since debut works are typically the most difficult items to acquire for any author, the most obvious reason being that writing produced at the dawn of a promising career is usually issued in small editions, and thus more difficult to locate years later once a reputation has been secured. My copies of *The Assistant, A New Life, The Fixer, The Tenants, Dubin's Lives,* and *God's Grace,* Malamud's subsequent novels, are all in superb condition, and each one boasts a crisp, immaculate dust jacket; whenever I see a copy of *The Natural* at a book fair or listed in a catalog, it is always priced well beyond my means, and thus it happened that I was thrilled to find, at Book Den East on Martha's Vineyard, a first in sound shape, but without the wrapper. I bought it for $20, and it remains on my shelves, a hedge against the day I find a better copy that I can afford. The last time I checked, two copies in what could be described as collectible condition were being offered, both of them by Ken Lopez of Hadley, Massachusetts. One copy, quoted at $3,750, was described as being "very nice," a qualification, Lopez explained in his description, that took note of its "lightly bumped" spine and a "small abrasion" to the "front pastedown." Another "near fine" copy was quoted at $15,000, the higher price justified by Malamud's inscription to a former colleague at Oregon State University, where he taught for twelve years. Either way, the likelihood that I will be stepping up in quality on this particular title any time soon is remote at best, although hope springs eternal, which is one of the enduring charms of collecting. Meanwhile, I am doing just fine with my au naturel copy of *The Natural.*

How a person goes about determining what is "collector's condition" is another matter entirely, especially when the book in question is a First Folio that is almost four hundred years old. The words of U.S. Supreme Court Justice Potter Stewart on the matter of deciding what is pornography and what is not—"I know it when I see it"—seem appropriate in this regard. As we have seen, there are categories that are applied frequently in the book trade, and they are helpful as a generic point of reference, particularly when talking about books published after 1900, but even then, experience—and an extra measure of street smarts—are qualities that can make all the difference in the world. It is not necessary for me to go through an exhaustive rundown of the various phrases dealers use to describe books. That is handled capably in many good references, a number of which are recommended elsewhere in the pages of this book, including several excellent websites for collectors that I have found useful, most commendably one set up and maintained as a public service by a collector, Steve Trussel, at www.trussel.com/f books. Another site offering similar features is www.resinets.com/topics/books, and for a comprehensive listing, and locator, of book sales throughout the United States, take a look at www.book-sales-in-america.com/.

Still, a brief commentary on the use of terms in general might be productive at this point, particularly with regard to the descriptions booksellers use to indicate the shape a book is in, and what is really meant when they are encountered by the book hunter. Only by spending time "out there"— going to book fairs, handling the goods, taking mental stock of what is being offered for sale—will a person get a feel for the degrees of quality that are actually meant. By far the most overused word in the bookseller's lexicon is *mint*, a decidedly nonbibliographic term that has no place in the trade, and should raise suspicions whenever it is encountered in a catalog or on a website. At least one prominent dealer, Kevin MacDonnell of Austin, Texas, admits to "going ballistic" whenever he sees his colleagues use the term. "Unlike books or glassware, coins are minted and made at a mint," he says. "A coin in mint condition is in the same condition as it was when it left the mint where it was made. Books are not minted, nor are they made in mints. But books were once 'new' and saying 'as new' I think better conveys the very best condition that a book can be in."

As a general rule, especially when dealing with twentieth-century books, a good piece of advice is to pay close attention to books that are described by reputable dealers to be *as new, very fine, near fine,* or *fine,* and to bear in mind that these phrases do not mean what people new to collecting typically think they should mean. According to guidelines adopted by the Antiquarian Booksellers Association of America, a book described as *very good* does not come close to being what common usage would lead you to believe those words should mean; the going definition for that category is "some wear, but no major defects." A book listed as *good,* by extension, really means that it is terrible, no two ways about it, and *fair,* quite frankly, really means poor, while *poor* refers to a book that should be used simply as a reading copy, and not considered as collectible except for the rarest of items, in which case condition itself becomes an irrelevant concept. The very best dealers will go beyond the catchphrases to offer an honest description of a book that accurately indicates the true physical health of the volume.

A question that logically arises from all of this might be

the following: Should a nascent bibliophile only consider books that are in pristine condition? Let me answer by offering a description of two books that the vast majority of collectors would dismiss on first glance as sadly tattered examples of common titles that have little value as literary works in great shape, let alone those that are deplorable. The first time I ever heard of Asa Gray's *Manual of the Botany of the Northern United States* also happened to be the first time I saw a copy of the book. I was visiting Middlebury College in Middlebury, Vermont, and was being given a tour of the rare-books section by the director of the division, Robert Buckeye. We were in the Robert Frost Room, and Buckeye withdrew from a metal file cabinet a package of what appeared, to all intents and purposes, to be a plastic bag filled with spare parts. What it actually contained was a book in several detached sections, and to say it had been read to death would have been an understatement. Published in 1848, this copy of a book commonly known as Gray's *Botany* had been the primary source of information for Henry David Thoreau's natural history writings, most notably *A Week on the Concord and Merrimack Rivers*, published a year later, in 1849. In an excellent essay titled "Thoreau as Botanist," the Harvard scholar Ray Angelo writes that this work, a manual for the identification of vascular plants, mosses, and liverworts of the northeastern United States, "heralded the end of a long period during which New England botany had languished at a relatively rudimentary level," and was responsible for having "directly crystallized Thoreau's botanical inclinations."

The copy of this book, bearing the authenticated ownership signature "H. D. Thoreau" on the front flyleaf, has obvious associative value as an artifact, but as Buckeye readily pointed out, there is nothing in and of itself that would assist a scholar's inquiries into the evolution of Thoreau's work that could not be obtained from another copy. "There are no annotations by Thoreau, so if you want to study the influence of the book on his writing, you can look at any other copy, and it is not an uncommon book." The significance of the Middlebury copy, in other words, is artifactual, even iconic to those who regard Thoreau as a thinker of consequence. "This is a book that I always show people who insist that condition is everything, when in cases like this, it is not a factor at all," Buckeye said.

A year or so after I was given that introduction to Gray's *Botany*, I was in Washington, D.C., to give a talk at the Center for the Book of the Library of Congress, when Clark W. Evans, senior reference librarian, graciously offered to show me some of the lesser-known treasures kept among the institution's 121 million objects. My eyes were drawn immediately to the ugly duckling of the selection, because I thought this little book had to have been brought out by mistake; it was in terrible shape, it was by no means attractive, it wasn't even a first edition. The lengthy title—*English Grammar in Familiar Lectures, Accompanied by a Compendium; Embracing a New Systematick Order of Parsing, a New System of Punctuation, Exercises in False Syntax, and a Key to the Exercise: Designed for the use of Schools and Private Learners*—offered no obvious clues as to its significance either.

Written by Samuel Kirkham, the book is known familiarly as Kirkham's *Grammar* and was immensely influential throughout the nineteenth century, so popular that a later search of the Harvard University on-line database indicated that it had gone through no fewer than 105 printings over a thirty-year period. First published in 1823, the copy I was being shown was a sixth edition that had been printed in 1828 in Cincinnati, Ohio. As the final eight words of the full title suggest—*for the use of Schools and Private Learners*—this book was especially favored by do-it-yourself students. The Library of Congress copy reflects uncounted hours of concentrated use. It is shabby, dull, and falling apart; clearly, it has been read, handled, and pored over assiduously by its prior owners. Inside the front cover, on a sheet known as the pastedown, is the signature of Abraham Lincoln, and what I was holding in my hands, Evans informed me, was the earliest extant book known to have been in the possession of the sixteenth president of the United States, a man whose formal education ended at first grade, a voracious reader who is faithfully reported to have walked twelve miles in 1830 to acquire this very book from a farmer, and to have worked a full day in return to pay for it. Because Lincoln was self-educated, it is not far-fetched to muse that the language skills he developed during these crucial years were honed with the help of Kirkham's *Grammar,* and that creation of the eloquent documents that lay ahead of him—the Emancipation Proclamation, the Gettysburg Address, the First and Second Inaugural Addresses among them—were influenced in no small way by this tattered primer.

How this fragile book became a part of the national collection is another story, one that also adds to its mystique, since also written on the title page, in Lincoln's hand, is a playful notation that "Ann M. Rutledge is now learning grammar," presumably with the aid of this manual, which Lincoln presented as a gift to the daughter of an acquaintance in New Salem, the same woman believed to be the sweetheart of his youth. Tragically, Ann Rutledge died in 1835, and the book passed on through members of her family, finally being tracked down in the 1920s by a woman named Jane Hammong, a Lincoln collector who turned it over to the nation as a gift. The Library of Congress has many dazzling Lincoln items in its collections, more than sixteen thousand items at last count, but none speak more eloquently, I think, than this essential text from his youth. So does condition matter? Is the copy flawed because it is a sixth edition and not a first? The answers to both questions quite obviously of course are no, it does not matter in the slightest.

In the case of these two books—Gray's *Botany* and Kirkham's *Grammar*—knowing great condition from forgettable condition is not a factor at all in determining the significance of the objects, and I offer these examples to point out that no rule is hard and fast, no axiom so sacrosanct that it can't be axed. There are collectors, in fact, who go after books that betray the scars of their existence. I think in particular of Jay Fliegelman, a collector of books known as association copies, who points to the tattered leaves of some books as proof of their incessant handling. In the case of the collector Michael Zinman, the existence of the artifact itself is far more relevant than condition, since so many of the obscure items he has sought out—specimens, in many cases, printed in the "cradle" period of the American colonies—exist in no other known instance, and he is grateful to have any examples of them at all, regardless of the wear and tear they may have endured over the decades. It is in this spirit of preservation, in fact, that Zinman formulated what he christened the *critical mess* theory of collecting, an approach that involves the casting out of a very wide net, and the consideration of everything that comes back in with "the catch of the day." Price, for the most part, is not an overriding factor of concern in this method either, since so much of the material being acquired is regarded as dead weight by the party putting it up for sale, and is offered more often than not with the idea of clearing out an eyesore and freeing up storage space than it is with the hope of turning a tidy profit. Zinman has collected in this manner for several decades, sometimes acquiring huge lots of material that are outside the limits of his primary interest, simply, in his words, "because the quantity and the dollars seemed reasonable at the time."

I have told the story elsewhere of how Zinman bought a massive archive of pornographic literature published between 1950 and 1975, not because he was in any way interested in the content, but because of those very reasons—it was there, and it was cheap. Trying later to get rid of the material without letting anyone know he had acquired it in the first place, the Ardsley, New York, collector donated what had become an embarrassment to the University of Texas Law School at Austin, which promptly established the Zinman Collection of Pornography in his name. "The point is that you must always be alert to the possibilities," Zinman said. "Nothing is junk, as far as I am concerned, nothing printed on paper is garbage." Zinman's dedication to this principle was reaffirmed in 1998 when he let it be known, to the dismay of officials at the New York Public Library, that he had acquired thousands of ephemeral materials from its collections that had been disbound at the spine ("guillotined" is the operative word), microfilmed as single sheets, and then sold to a broker who deals in scrap paper. The controversy that followed in the aftermath of the disclosures prompted the library to issue new guidelines governing the preservation of all materials, and to terminate the process of cutting up rarities in order to copy their content.

It is collecting material like this, in fact, that suggests so many possibilities to the book hunter of the twenty-first century, and there are numerous models to emulate. Diana Korzenik, a retired art instructor in Massachusetts, spent the better part of thirty years scouring the flea markets and antique shops of New England seeking out every manner of instructional object that had been used by teachers in the nineteenth century during the Industrial Revolution. "These were in junk boxes," Korzenik told me, indicating a mass of art supply catalogs, pattern books, pasting books, drawing cards, and glass slates she had gathered in her countless "ferreting expeditions" throughout the region. Many of them she had never seen or heard of before and never encountered again. A good deal of the objects were ephemeral items not intended by their creators to last forever, but which now, by their very scarcity, provide revealing windows on a particular time and place, lending insight into how a theory of American education was put into practice more than a century ago.

Korzenik paid on average five to twenty dollars each for these objects, and used them as the basis for several monographs that she wrote, referring to them often in the courses she taught at Massachusetts Institute of Art and Harvard University. When she retired in 1996, she presented the material to the Huntington Library in San Marino, California, with an appraised value of two hundred thousand dollars, creating in an instant an archive of nineteenth-century artifacts that is of particular interest to researchers. Not unlike the great collection of Confederate imprints gathered by the historian Francis Parkman in the closing years of the Civil War for the Boston Athenæum, the Korzenik Collection—and the Michael Zinman Collection of Early American Imprints now installed at the Library Company of Philadelphia—is measured by the totality of the materials, not by the market value of individual items. It is for this reason, more than any other, that a clear plan of exactly what it is a collector wants to accomplish is essential, and the earlier a scope is determined—or when a focus, in the jargon of the cognoscenti, is established—the better. "There are all sorts of book collectors, probably as many as there are kinds of allergies," Colton Storm and Howard Peckham wrote in *Invitation to Book Collecting,* a 1947 introduction to prospective participants. For their purposes, the distinction was limited to "those with a proper and high regard for the art" of the activity, "except on certain occasions when our scorn for some inferior book gourmands will be quite obvious." In this rather elitist paradigm, connoisseurship is what matters most of all, a quality that "implies an exercise of the mind through the use of the senses." In that instance, at least, we are in agreement.

Once a person has formulated an idea of what it is that is being undertaken—it can be literary, historical, documentary, graphic, unique to a particular time, place, activity, profession—then comes the matter of acquiring expertise. Before long comes something else, the skill to know the good from the not-so-good, a kind of intuitive comprehension that develops in time. I once asked the legendary pilot Chuck Yeager what makes a great aviator—what quality he wanted more than anything else, in other words, in a wingman who would be flying combat missions with him and "watching his sixes," as the professionals say—and the answer was instantaneous: "Hours," he said. "How much time has the guy logged in the cockpit, at that stick." Experience, in other words, the repetition of maneuvers, the honing of subtle skills, the sharpening of reflexes, and the perfection of finesse, but experience all the same.

The veteran New York booksellers Leona Rostenberg and Madeleine Stern use a German expression, *Fingerspitzengefühl,* to explain what it is that helps them recognize important material when they encounter it, even if what they find happens to be material they have never heard of before they pick it up for the first time. "This is how you know a rare book when you see one," Rostenberg told me as she rubbed the thumbs of both her hands against her forefingers, and thereupon described an "electric tingling" that runs from the volume being handled, up the arm, and into the consciousness. Part instinct, perhaps, part intuition, the ability to "feel" the significance of a book may move some skeptics to compare the exercise being described to being little more than learning how to pick ripe tomatoes out of a vegetable bin at a farmer's market. One of the most accomplished collectors of Americana alive, a retired Beverly Hills dentist named Dr. Gary Milan, identified the ultimate tool in his hunt for rare collectibles by holding up *his* two hands, and turning them around for me to see. "A dentist works with these," he said. "A dentist *feels,* and with me, everything begins with touch." Milan also said that to be the best at what he does, he buys, on average, one reference book for every two or three collectibles he acquires, and that it takes a "killer instinct" to beat out the competition consistently, but that's another tale for another time. My point here is that cultivating every one of the five senses is not much different from logging a lot of hours in the cockpit, only with books there remains an added dimension, which Rostenberg described as well as anyone. "More important than anything," she emphasized, "is that you love books."

Other respected book people—the Paris bookseller Pierre Berès comes immediately to mind—report a similar chemistry at work. "When I enter a room," he told me, "I find I know exactly what is there," even if the room has been untouched for decades. "I feel I know exactly what the contents are." Like Rostenberg and Stern, Berès described a physical response that takes place with every book he handles, a process just as meaningful as engaging with it intellectually. He commences what he called a "promenade" with every book he encounters, and he described the reaction he has in terms that would sound alien to most amateur book people, even ludicrous to some. "You have to sleep with the book, to live with the book," he said in total seriousness. "You must handle the book, you must not to be afraid to have intimate contact with the book." For Heribert Tenschert, the renowned German dealer in medieval and Renaissance manuscripts, unique items hundreds of years old that often sell for sums in seven figures, the process is no different, even the heat of the passion is similar. "When I get offered a book, I see it, I feel it, I browse through it," he told me. "I smell it. I get in touch with it. And then I buy it." The renowned American bookseller of the mid-twentieth century, Dr. A. S. W. Rosenbach of Philadelphia, went so far as to claim greater satisfaction from handling books than indulging in "the physical act of love."

Nobody is suggesting that the bibliophile must abjure all earthly pleasures in order to achieve fulfillment as a book hunter. What these veteran practitioners are saying, however, is that there is no substitute for touch. Collectors are tactile people, and for all the wonders of the Internet and the millions of databases that can be accessed through its spellbinding search engines, a person still has to handle the goods in order to achieve full satisfaction. It is no coincidence that all of the actions associated with book collecting are erotically charged. You caress the binding gently and with soft strokes, you become dizzy by the lustrous texture of the paper and are left weak-kneed by the bite of the type. On first embrace, you fill your lungs with a fragrance so intoxicating that it has the energy of a thrilling liaison, and when it is time to reflect on the triumph, you glow with the knowledge that you have acquitted yourself in a manner that just may have surpassed your wildest expectations. Should it come as any surprise that the great eighteenth-century lover of women, Giovanni Giacomo Casanova, was also a formidable bookman who spent the final years of his life as a librarian in Bohemia for a nobleman who had taken the impoverished count in and offered him shelter? A full generation before Sigmund Freud made people think twice about the subtleties of the sensual references they made in their casual conversation, the French bibliophile Octave Uzanne wrote how he would spend entire days by the bookstalls on the Quai Voltaire "taking delight" in the "pleasant touching" of books "long coveted," looking forward eagerly to the chance "to fondle a binding," all the while reveling in the secret "joys" that "the hand shares with the eye." He continues in this vein, but you get the point—a gentle madness, indeed.

CHAPTER 4

THREE LITTLE WORDS

Easily the most frequently used, and therefore the most frequently misused, words in book collecting are *rarity, scarcity,* and *value.* Sooner or later—and more often than not it is sooner—a series of questions are mulled over haphazardly, if not asked outright, by anyone who has begun to build a private library. They go something like this: Is it true that I am investing my time, energy, and resources in pursuit of things that are rare, and therefore likely to be worth a considerable amount of money? If that happens to be the case, is it fair to assume that these things are rare because they are scarce, or merely because a lot of people want what only a few of us can have? Leaving adjectives aside for the moment, we are then moved to wonder if the value of this material is something that can be measured on the basis of a uniform standard, which leads to a related question, to wit: Is *value* something that should be determined on the basis of dollars and cents alone, or is there a deeper ingredient—*worth,* and all that implies—that ought to be layered into the mix as well?

Since the casual observer generally considers people who collect old books synonymous with people who covet rare books, in essence regarding the two qualities as one and the same, it may be a good idea to start there. For the compilers of dictionaries, *rarity* defines the fairly straightforward condition of being uncommon, though occasionally the word implies excellence. Both of these are good words, and they can, and very often do, apply to books, though excellence does involve another word that crops up frequently—*taste*—and the shaping of a judgment that involves a subjective point of view. Still, with books, there are further subtleties all the same, as John Carter attempted to explain in *A B C for Book Collectors,* a manual of 450 bibliographic expressions, first issued in 1952 and now in its seventh edition and still regarded as the primary handbook of technical terms for the pastime. Not surprisingly, the longest entry in the book, two and a half pages, is devoted to *rarity,* which Carter coyly described as the "salt" in book collecting, and by that he meant "if you take too much" the flavor of the dish is spoiled, and "if you take too neat it will make you sick." Like everyone else who has considered the word as it applies to artifacts, Carter danced around its true meaning, quoting a number of his friends and colleagues on the matter. I particularly like the description he included from the late American collector Robert H. Taylor, who said, simply, that a rare book is "a book I want badly and can't find," though there is added merit to Paul Angle's nuanced qualification of stressing "important" alongside "desirable and hard to get." For his

part, Carter offered a number of categories—*absolute rarity,*
relative rarity, temporary rarity, and *localized rarity,* niceties
that need little elaboration here, except to say that each deals
in varying degrees with supply and demand.

The larger point, I think, is that too much is made about
whether a book is rare or not, because it does tend to muddy
the waters somewhat over the true goal of the exercise, which
is to put something together that creates a whole, something,
at the risk of being repetitive, that creates a compelling narrative. If done with sufficient panache and thought, what
results will not only be rare, it will be unique, and extremely
satisfying as well. On the matter of determining scarcity, perhaps the most salient example involves the First Folio of
Shakespeare, arguably the greatest book ever printed in the
English language, and as we discussed in chapter 3, certainly
among the most highly coveted. While it goes without saying
that any book that sells for $6.16 million on the open market
is expensive, that fact alone does not necessarily mean that it
is scarce or, for that matter, necessarily rare. Confused? Consider this: According to the most recent census published by
Oxford University Press, 228 known copies of the First Folio
of Shakespeare remain in the world, 80 of them alone in the
collections of the Folger Shakespeare Library in Washington,
D.C. Although no business records of the seventeenth-century
London printer Isaac Jaggard survive, it is believed this number—70 more, incidentally, than were known to exist in a
census compiled just a century ago—represents perhaps a
quarter of the copies printed, a circumstance, if true, that
would not make it particularly *uncommon* in any conventional sense of the word. What it does imply is that the importance of the book was recognized immediately upon its

appearance, and that it has never even come close to extinction. To suggest further, however, that because the book is not scarce means that it therefore is not rare would be ridiculous. In this sense, rarity is achieved by a combination of *significance, desirability,* and *availability,* not forgetting the iconic nature of the book's miraculous existence, and in the case of the Berland copy sold at Christie's in October 2001, the matchless condition and impeccable provenance that made it irresistible to those few who could afford the luxury of even considering its ownership. Similar details apply to the book commonly called the Gutenberg Bible, also known as the 42-Line Bible and for many years also the Mazarine Bible in honor of Cardinal Mazarin, a famous early owner; more significantly, it is universally acknowledged to be the first work printed in Europe from movable type, and for that detail alone it is of supreme cultural significance. Once again, no production records exist of its creation, none of the original type survives, and of the printer himself, only a severely truncated biographical sketch of his life has come down to our time. Information on how many copies were produced is not known, but the best educated guess says something perhaps on the order of two hundred sets, most printed on handmade paper, a more elegant version on vellum. Today, there are twenty-two known complete copies in various collections around the world, with another copy that has been unaccounted for since 1945; twenty-four other copies have missing leaves. Of these forty-seven copies, twelve were printed on vellum, and only four—those at the Library of Congress, the British Library, the Bibliothèque Nationale, and Göttingen University Library—are complete. So is this a scarce book? Relatively speaking, no. There are four times as many Gutenberg Bibles in the world as there are copies of the Bay Psalm Book of 1639. But its rarity is such that it would have to be regarded as being by far the most coveted printed book in the world.

The recently concluded bibliographical survey of Nicolaus Copernicus's monumental sixteenth-century book, *De revolutionibus orbium coelestium* (On the Revolutions of Heavenly Spheres), by the renowned Harvard-Smithsonian astronomer Dr. Owen Gingerich, is a heroic example of one person's dedication to learn as much as humanly possible about every known copy of a particular book—in this case a work that verily shook the heavens by proposing the theretofore preposterous notion that the earth revolves around the sun, not the other way around. Dr. Gingerich, a noted bibliophile I have had the pleasure of interviewing on several occasions, spent three decades traveling the globe on an inspired mission to examine firsthand every known first and second edition copy of the pathbreaking book. Emboldened by a single phrase—Dr. Gingerich told me he wanted to disprove an assertion he had read somewhere that *De revolutionibu*s was "the greatest book *never* read"—he examined 580 sixteenth-century copies in libraries scattered throughout Europe and North America, as well as those in China and Japan, looking over every one for telling annotations from the earliest readers, and recording every pertinent physical detail through an exacting process of bibliographic examination known as *collation*. His annotated census of these books was published in 2002 as a 434-page monograph. In recognition of these continued studies, Dr. Gingerich was awarded the Polish government's Order of Merit in 1981, and more recently an asteroid has been named in his honor.

That more than five hundred copies of a book published in 1543 should survive is amazing enough, but what is truly remarkable is just how valuable the book is on the open market. Without exception, every great collector of science I have met—the late Dr. Haskell Norman, whose library of medicine and science sold at Sotheby's in 1997 for $18.6 million comes immediately to mind—has unhesitatingly asserted that the one book they have craved above all others—the word *lust* would not be inappropriate—is a Copernicus, which is why prices of four hundred thousand dollars are not uncommon, and why this book, perhaps more than any other in recent years, has been the target of so many thefts around the world. Once again we see rarity and scarcity, supply and demand coming into play, and they are combined with all the other factors that go into making a particular book *great,* in this instance involving a category of book that could be said to have "changed the world" in a palpable way. It was this very premise, "changing the world," that shaped the collection of the James Bond novelist, Ian Fleming, and which in 1963 occasioned one of the most influential book exhibitions of modern times, *Printing and the Mind of Man.* Today, the descriptive catalog of that show is a highly collectible item in its own right, with prices of two hundred dollars routinely quoted for decent copies and much more for those in fine condition.

When a book was printed is a factor in a number of instances as well. So often importance is attached, a degree of scholarly respect is assumed, by virtue of a book's *age.* But from a collector's point of view, there really has to be something about a book beyond the fact that it is old to make it worth owning. This should be pretty obvious, but it remains the greatest misconception held by people just starting out as book hunters, the belief that just because something has survived the passage of a considerable period of time makes it rare, scarce, or at the very least desirable. More often than not the day of true epiphany comes when a Bible that has been in a family for generations is brought to a dealer for appraisal. What is learned quickly enough is that the value of a book that millions and millions of people own—assuming, of course, that it is not, say, an Eliot Indian Bible of 1661, or a Douay Bible of 1790—is personal, and not monetary, regardless of how old it is.

Anyone who grasps these basic components can begin to understand the principles at work in book collecting. Although age, as I have suggested, does not necessarily guarantee rarity, there are some qualifications that must be mentioned. Any printed book, for example, that was produced in the 1400s is known as an incunable or incunabulum, both variations of the same word, and derivations of a Latin phrase meaning "from the cradle," and used to identify books issued in this embryonic period. It has been estimated that as many as 10 million books came off the presses of Europe during that fifty-year period, 1450 through 1500, with an estimated two hundred thousand or so that are believed to have survived the passage of five and half centuries to our time. Regardless of the content they might have, each and every one of these surviving books is rare for the simple fact of its having successfully navigated the hazards endemic to any half-a-millennium journey through time. Some of these survivors, needless to say, are going to be more precious than others by dint of what they are and what they contain, but it is still valid to assert that if it is an incunable, it is a rare book, regardless of the content. By way of extension, any-thing printed in North America from the establishment of the first press in Cambridge, Massachusetts, in 1639 through the end of 1800 are uniformly important; some notable collec-tors of Americana, like Michael Zinman of Ardsley, New York, whose substantial collection of imprints are now installed at the Library Company of Philadelphia, call these earliest pieces from the seventeenth century "American incun-ables."

Age apart from content matters to varying degrees else-where as well, a situation that has become apparent in recent years with regard to the way libraries around the world are deciding which titles they will keep in their collections, and which ones should either be "preserved" through deacidifica-tion processes, copied onto microfilm, "guillotined," and digitized, or discarded altogether. In the United States, a non-profit group called the Task Force on the Artifact in the Library of the Future was established in 1999 by the Council on Library and Information Resources to set appropriate guidelines. "Where we come in," Dr. Stephen G. Nichols, chairman of the group, told me shortly after assuming the position, "is what happens after 1800, since anything printed before that date, by general scholarly convention, has been established to be important, and worthy of preservation for that fact in and of itself."

How this view impacts the collector comes with the know-ledge that any book printed prior to the nineteenth century is considered by the academic community to be worth preserv-ing in a scholarly sense, merely by virtue of its existence as an historical artifact. In a draft report issued late in 2001, the task force listed a number of criteria it had settled on to evaluate the merits of any other books, regardless of when they were printed. These categories are useful to know in that they parallel in many ways the kinds of factors collectors and dealers take into account when they are assessing various titles. They are *age, evidential value, aesthetic value, scarcity, associational value, market value,* and *exhibition value.* As a further point of departure, the compilers of the report offered this observation:

> The value of the artifact for research purposes—as opposed to its monetary value or exhibition value—is chiefly evidentiary. An artifact is of evidential value because it testifies to the extent the information in it is original, faithful, fixed, or stable.

As far as the collector is concerned, the key difference here is that evidential value is not the same as monetary value. For example, a pamphlet could survive in one or two copies, a likelihood that is not unusual and in fact is encountered all the time, yet because the item is so obscure and so arcane it stimulates no competitive demand—nobody wants it, in other words—it is not of sufficient interest to command a dear price in the marketplace. Does that in any way diminish its importance as an historical artifact, something that a scholar or researcher might find interesting at some point in the future? The obvious answer is that it does not. But the larger point here is that scarcity does not necessarily ensure rarity, and rarity is not synonymous with scarcity. *Absolute rarity,* as defined by John Carter, is an instance where we know that only a very small number of copies were produced, which is why the first books of important authors of any century are typically the most difficult to acquire, since they are for the most part unknown when first issued because of limited public demand, and therefore produced in small quantities. In cases where first books also become signature books—*Look Homeward, Angel, The Catcher in the Rye, To Kill a Mockingbird, Catch-22, The Moviegoer, Gone with the Wind, One Flew over the Cuckoo's Nest* come immediately to mind—first issue copies in fine condition become all the more desirable, much more difficult to locate, and therefore command the highest prices among literary works of the nineteenth and twentieth centuries.

"Your collection must be worth a fortune" is an oft-expressed comment uttered by the uninitiated, and collectors do little to dismiss that perception by boasting every now and then about how much someone else's copy of a book they bought ten or fifteen years ago just realized at a Swann Galleries auction, especially if the sum is in the middle five figures. Why we persist in doing ill-advised things like that is beyond me; maybe it is because we need to be reassured that we really aren't jeopardizing the family's financial stability by investing in books, that we've actually been shrewd with our purchases. It is said, in fact, that the reason Arthur Houghton Jr., one of the great American collectors of the twentieth century and the principal benefactor of the Houghton Library of rare books and manuscripts at Harvard University, chose to sell his fabulous collection of European high spots in 1976 was so that he could sit at the back of the auction gallery while millions of dollars were being bid on his books, and prove to everyone who ever said he was crazy that he knew very well what he had been doing with his money all the time. This persistent discussion—of whether or not a collector is spending wisely—brings to mind another loathsome phrase, *disposable income,* that should be retired permanently, since by definition anyone who has money to dispose of is throwing it away. My feeling is that anyone who throws money away on worthless books is not collecting wisely or intelligently in the first place, and is going about the process with a flawed attitude. For pure simplicity, the best working definition of an antiquarian book that I know of is the one suggested by Bart Auerbach, a Manhattan appraiser and consultant for Sotheby's book and manuscript department: "It is a book that is worth more money now than when it was published." That dictum rather neatly accounts for all the variables and keeps things in perspective.

At the other extreme, let it also be said that if you become a player with an idea toward securing a substantial return on a wise investment, good for you, but you are on your own as far as I am concerned, because this isn't about making money, it is about gratifying a passion in a sensible way. At the end of the day, if you have gone about the task prudently, you just may come out ahead, but financial advice is the purview of portfolio advisers, not bibliophiles. Having said that, let it also be said that like all good investments, a good rule of thumb with books is to buy what you know, and to proceed with due diligence in areas that are unfamiliar to you. Sounds straightforward enough, but buying blind seems to be the most frequently committed transgression in book collecting.

With that caveat firmly on the record, it must also be stressed that one of the exquisite charms of book collecting is that anyone can play. It is a game for the very wealthy, of that there is no doubt, and the truth is that we occasionally become benumbed by some of the prices people pay for books. I am as guilty of this kind of voyeurism as anyone, and I make no apologies for reporting in my books the fascination so many of us have demonstrated for the hunt for big game. But I have also taken tremendous satisfaction in pointing out instances where some really wonderful collections—truly *great* collections, in fact—have been put together on modest budgets and with limited means. Let's face it, knowing what the stuff is going to cost you, and what it really is worth, is central to the exercise. To that end, it behooves the collector to know how it is that prices are determined, and how to run price checks before committing to a purchase.

In the area of modern literature, Americana, early printed books, mysteries, science fiction, children's books, natural history, photography, and travel, by far the best one-volume summary of prices is *Collected Books: The Guide to Values,* which in 2002 was released in a third, totally updated edition, and reflects retail prices that were current the previous year. The key point for collectors to appreciate is the word *retail;* the compilers of the guide, Allen and Patricia Ahearn, draw their data from numerous sources, most notably prices paid at auction and prices quoted in dealers' catalogs and listed on-line at their websites. Their figures are tabulated to suggest what a person might expect to pay for a particular title, not what a person might realize in the sale of the same item to a dealer, or even if consigned to an auction house, since it is dealers who typically buy at sales, a process they undertake with the idea of turning a profit in later transactions.

What the Ahearns offer, and indeed what the compilers of other handbooks offer, is a guide based on prevailing prices, and they furnish *issue points,* where applicable, to help collectors determine whether or not a book is, in fact, a *first edition* and everything that exalted designation implies. One of my favorite examples, since it is the first actual issue point determination I made "in the field" with a book of substance—one I had just found on Martha's Vineyard—Nathaniel Hawthorne's *Scarlet Letter* (1850)—requires that the word *reduplicate* appear on line 20 of page 21 instead of *repudiate*. If you have that point in your copy, and if the book is still bound in its original brown cloth, then you are talking in the neighborhood of ten thousand dollars. Even finer distinctions apply for John Steinbeck's *Of Mice and Men* (1937), with several points separating the first edition, first issue, from the first edition, second issue; the former must have the phrase "and only moved because the heavy hands were pendula" on lines 20–21 of page 9. If you have a copy in fine condition—and that assumes the presence of an original dust jacket that is clean with only minimal soiling—the Ahearns say it can sell for up to thirty-five hundred dollars in today's market. Altogether there are twenty thousand entries like this in *Collected Books,* by no means every book the collector of modern first editions will be curious about investigating, but a superb reference all the same. Individual bibliographies abound for hundreds of writers, and are easily located through normal research methods. Since the unfortunate demise of *Biblio* and *AB Bookman's Weekly* magazines in 1999, the most useful periodical now published in the United States dealing with book collecting is *Firsts,* a monthly that frequently features checklists of important authors (see www.firsts.com). The best journal devoted to book collecting published in the English language on any continent remains *The Book Collector,* a quarterly founded in 1952 in London by the novelist-bibliophile Ian Fleming (see www.thebookcollector. co.uk) and edited for many years by Nicolas Barker.

There are other references to consult, many of them expensive to own, but readily available for consultation at most libraries. See the selected bibliography in the Appendix for my top choices. Any collector who aspires to the next level of expertise must inevitably become conversant with *American Book Prices Current* (ABPC), an annual record of books, manuscripts, autographs, maps, and broadsides sold at auction in North America, the United Kingdom, Germany, various European countries, and Australia. It is a standard reference used by dealers, appraisers, auction houses, scholars, and tax authorities. Established in 1895, ABPC has been owned since 1972 by a husband-wife team of bibliographer-historians, Daniel J. Leab and Katharine Kyes Leab, formerly based in New York, now in Washington, Connecticut. Each year they issue a one-volume compilation of verified auction results recorded during the previous year, providing the most reliable accounting of prices paid for literary material in open competition. Since 1994, the Leabs also have issued a CD-ROM that makes immediately accessible some eight hundred thousand records going back to 1975, an extraordinary resource with which to track the prices realized for materials in a striking variety of ways.

As editor of the annual for thirty years, Kathy Leab has witnessed firsthand a remarkable period in the history of book collecting. And as an enthusiastic student of the exercise, she has been in the position to form some interesting opinions not only on what has transpired, but what may well be forthcoming, particularly as bookselling becomes more and more dependent on the World Wide Web. "It seems to me that one way you get people interested in books is by getting them into libraries," she told me during a series of interviews conducted in 2002. "Much of what you see on the

Internet is what we call 'one-fool marketing,' which is based on the theory that there is one fool out there for every book, somebody who will pay an absurdly high price—and that's all you need to survive." By that standard alone, it is no great revelation to learn that Leab is not overly enthusiastic about the various ways on-line sales have impacted the book business, particularly in the way that they have, in her view, "dumbed down" the process. "Books tend to be more expensive on the Net, and everyone with an attic looks at the prices out there and thinks that's what they'll get for their copies. My point is that if you are really going to be serious about collecting or dealing, you have to know what auctions are all about, and to take the time to learn the fundamentals of what is going on."

The home page of the website maintained by the Leabs (www.bookpricescurrent.com) is among the best I've seen, not simply for the introduction it gives to their annual report, but also for the links it has to other useful sites and the informative essays it offers, and for the refreshing willingness to help the beginner it proclaims. The first statement that appears when logging on, in bold capital letters, is "individual questions cheerfully answered," an invitation few busy people are willing to make in an on-line world, much less feel obligated to honor when there is little likelihood that what comes in will generate any business.

Given the sophistication of her compilations, Leab is frequently asked whether or not the books and compact discs she and her husband produce are the kind of resource novice collectors ought to be buying, or if they should be doing a little introductory work beforehand. *American Book Prices Current* is not an inexpensive proposition, after all. The

2002 edition of the printed book was listed at $139; the CD-ROM, fully searchable from 1975 on, was quoted at $2,000, with annual updates furnished thereafter at $164 a year. "People call me on the phone, and I won't sell them *American Book Prices Current* unless they already have the basic tools like Carter [*A B C for Book Collectors*] and are acquainted with the basic bibliographies. For instance, if they are seriously interested in American literature, they should be familiar with BAL [*Bibliography of American Literature*]. I probably have sent more people to libraries, one by one, than any other living human being. If you assume that I am the ice-cream lady, then what I do is make them eat their dinner first."

Leab said she also likes to "beat the drum a lot" for Rare Book School (RBS), an independent, nonprofit, educational institute supporting the study of the history of books and printing and related subjects, and operated since 1992 at the University of Virginia in Charlottesville, where the founder and director, Dr. Terry Belanger, is university professor and honorary curator of special collections. Though located on a college campus, the forty courses are taught in five-day sequences without credit, and broadly directed toward antiquarian booksellers, collectors, bookbinders, conservators, teachers, and avocational students of the history of books and printing. Other classes are designed for research and rare-book librarians, archivists, and curators. In 2002, the cost for each five-day course was $745, with admissions granted on a rolling basis. Courses include such titles as Advanced Descriptive Bibliography, Electronic Texts & Images, Book Illustration Processes to 1890, European Decorative Bookbinding, How to Research a Rare Book, and a basic introduction to Book Collecting.

Obviously, RBS may be too much for the most casual of hobbyists, but it provides unique opportunities, and the reading lists are posted at the Rare Book School website (www.virginia.edu/old/books), along with summary descriptions of every course, a superb resource in its own right that is immediately available to anyone who cares to log on. The faculty Belanger has assembled includes some of the foremost professionals in the world. I know several enthusiasts who were "amateurs" when they participated in the program, and all sing its praises. John Robinson Block, editor in chief and copublisher of the *Toledo Blade* and *Pittsburgh Post-Gazette,* two family-owned newspapers, who has become a serious player in the field of Americana, enrolled at RBS simply because he wanted to become a more knowledgeable book collector, and he has returned for several sessions. Another recent graduate, Nick Aretakis, took several courses while working as a television producer for C-SPAN in Washington, D.C., and "thinking about a career change." He is now working full-time with the bookseller Bill Reese in New Haven, Connecticut.

"I like Rare Book School a great deal because it is the only place I know of where collectors, dealers, librarians, archivists, bibliographers, *anybody* interested in books, can meet other people who are *not* like themselves," Leab said. "And it is a wonderful place because you learn unexpected things. You can be anybody at all, and you'll meet and exchange ideas with many different people. There are times when I think it is the last best hope for preserving this rare-books culture we love so dearly."

Having handled nearly a million auction records over three decades, Leab is in an ideal position to comment on the rare-book market at its most fundamental level, the transfer of valuable material by way of open bidding. "One basic observation I can make is that price and value are not identical concepts," she made clear, addressing herself to a historic point of contention that never strays too far from the discourse. "I believe that value in terms of *intellectual* value or *artistic* value is not necessarily equivalent to what an object *costs,* and this can vary from field to field. If you're dealing with botanicals, price is determined by the quality of the illustrations; if you are dealing with the history of the computer, it may be in the scarcity of a mimeographed manual that almost everybody threw away, and is now what everybody wants to have. Obviously, people very much *do* want to know what the price of something is going to be, and they are interested in how it has fluctuated over the years, and that is something they can track with our data. For people just starting out, it is important, first of all, to build the best intellectual picture that you can have of what it is that is about to consume your attention and then to build the best collection you can. At some point, price absolutely does become important, because you don't want to be a fool in buying as in selling. It is always interesting to me that some books are not valuable simply because people keep them. I am always asked about a certain book about the sinking of the *Titanic* that will never have any value because thousands of them were printed right after the ship sank in 1912, and nobody ever threw any copy of it away. Every copy was saved; they're all still *out there*—they're everywhere—so there's no absolute scarcity. There isn't even any relative scarcity, there's nothing, and they're all in splendid condition. When the movie came out, hundreds of people wrote us, thinking they owned a 'hot' item. Probably 90 percent of them have been unable to sell the book at all."

For her part, Leab finds great drama in the galleries of the auction houses, and believes that electronic trading will never be a substitute for the experience. "Bookselling is theater, and that is something the Internet cannot duplicate. It cannot create the drama that the dealer or the auction fires up in a collector's mind." Leab said she does not include the results of on-line auctions in her compilations, and will not until there is a "live component" at work in the competition. "Fair market value is determined by a willing buyer and a willing seller, and you cannot determine that in an on-line auction because you cannot see the process. You don't know whether or not the final bidder is in fact the last person who would have placed a bid, or even if there are real bidders at all. There are photos posted of the books in some instances, but a photo is still a two-dimensional object, it's flat; you can see what it is, but flaws can be doctored up. The problem is the 'piggery-pokery' aspect—the pig in the poke. There has to be an opportunity at some physical location to see the book, unless it is a low-value item you want for research or sentimental value."

Another difficulty some professionals have with on-line auctions, especially those mounted on www.eBay.com, is the total absence of accountability on the part of the auction house. This shortcoming is made immediately evident to everyone who signs up for a password to either bid on material or to offer it for sale. The eBay disclaimer states that even though the company is "commonly referred to as an on-line auction website, it is important to realize that we are not a traditional 'auctioneer,'" emphasizing instead its role as a "venue" for all transactions. "We are not involved in the actual transaction between buyers and sellers. As a result, we have no control over the quality, safety, or legality of the items advertised, the truth or accuracy of the listings, the ability of sellers to sell items or the ability of buyers to buy items. We cannot ensure that a buyer or seller will actually complete a transaction." eBay, moreover, takes no responsibility for confirming the "purported identity" of buyers or sellers, and stresses, in capital letters, that everything is sold "'AS IS' AND WITHOUT ANY WARRANTY OR CONDITION, EXPRESS, IMPLIED OR STATUTORY."

Every dealer who is a member of a professional association of booksellers, on the other hand, be it the Antiquarian Booksellers Association of America, the various international groups, and all of the regional organizations, subscribes to a written code of ethics that governs the way they do business, and imposes sanctions in cases of extreme violations. A telling example is the second rule listed by ABAA: "An Association member shall be responsible for the accurate description of all material offered for sale. All significant defects, restorations, and sophistications should be clearly noted and made known to those to whom the material is offered or sold. Unless both parties agree otherwise, a full cash refund shall be made available to the purchaser of any misrepresented material."

Still, bidding for collectibles on eBay does have its exciting moments, and the free and easy nature of the systems is such that it cuts both ways, offering numerous opportunities for the knowledgeable collector who is alert to the badly perceived, totally misunderstood, and incompetently described items that crop up every so often. Reports are rampant of books being described as "first editions" when the items in question are actually worthless book club copies or reprint editions.

That the warning posted on the site is much more than a disclaimer required by lawyers surfaced on February 11, 2002, when an assistant U. S. attorney in Philadelphia announced the arrest of Shawn Aubitz, a fourteen-year employee of the National Archives, on charges of stealing dozens of historical documents and selling them to unwitting collectors and dealers on eBay. The thefts of no fewer than one hundred documents said to be worth at least one hundred thousand dollars were taken from the federal depository's field office in downtown Philadelphia between 1996 and 1999, and put up for sale on the Internet. The thefts came to light when a National Park Service employee called authorities after seeing an item on eBay and "becoming suspicious of the availability of the document," according to Robert Zauzmer of the federal prosecutor's office. The stolen items included pardons signed by James Madison, Abraham Lincoln, and Andrew Johnson, Civil War documents including an 1863 warrant to the United States Marshal to seize the estate of Robert E. Lee, and slave-trade documents. Aubitz was said to be cooperating with the Federal Bureau of Investigation, and sixty items were reported to have been recovered, "but many others were sold and have not been located."

As in every collecting endeavor, whether it be on-line or out in the field, the best advice is still *two* little words, not three—caveat emptor—buyer beware. They apply as much now as ever before.

CHAPTER 5

SPINNING A YARN

What some bibliophiles regard as a specialty, I like to think of as a theme. What some call focus, I prefer to call context. Such fine distinctions may well be little more than matters of taste, since both argue strongly for the development of a central plan, yet they support my considered view that every collector is a storyteller, and that every collection a form of narrative, a perspective that raises the process of forming a personal library above the pointless exercise of accumulation without direction. If you are inclined to accept this proposition, it follows that the plot line that emerges is as much a reflection of personality and purpose as it is of life experience. "A shelf of books bespeaks the soul whose hands have put it there" is the quaint way one collector, Minor Myers Jr., described the process for me; a bit studied, perhaps, but on point all the same. In his case, Myers—the president of Illinois

Wesleyan University, a historian, and an amateur musician—
was talking about the way his numerous passions express
themselves in the areas that he collects, the most curious
among them being the eighteenth century in all its glory: anything he can find, on any subject, that was published in the
1700s, anywhere in the world, with the single qualification
that it be "cheap." Another of his interests—the location and
acquisition of long-forgotten musical scores from the same
period—takes shape in the form of performance, with Myers
playing the compositions on his 1787 harpsichord, and gifted
students from the college's music department joining in on
other instruments. "That's the most exciting aspect of bringing home a pile of miscellaneous stuff," Myers explained.
"You don't really know what it is you have until you've had
a chance to sort through it all and see what is actually there."

The idea of having a focus in book collecting has the
weight of gospel, and you will get no murmur from me that
it is a flawed admonition. What I am trying to underscore is
that a person is well advised to keep an open mind, and to
always be receptive to the prospect of encountering things
that are *interesting,* if only because they add weight to material already in your possession. It goes without saying that if
you are a serious collector, then you have chosen a specialty,
you may well have several specialties, but you also have an
imagination, and if I am correct in suggesting that a collection is a form of storytelling, then the artifacts you have gathered become points of reference that tie the various strands
together, and give life to the narrative you are weaving. I
think in this regard of a wonderfully anachronistic institution founded by Thomas Carlyle in 1841 known as the London Library, where the continuing claim to distinction is the

magnificently idiosyncratic way material is assembled, and the humanistic system that is used to classify and shelve books, which at last count numbered just over 1 million volumes. For the readers who use the resources of the institution, what emerges from all this, according to the librarian, Alan Bell, is a stimulating process of foraging in the stacks that he calls associative browsing, exactly the kind of foraging that proves so delightfully productive in the fertile stomping grounds of the book hunter.

Having said that, let me also say that I am not advocating the creation of a cabinet of wonders, a menagerie of assorted trinkets that provides casual amusement to someone who has brought various knickknacks together and arranged them as curiosities in a glass case. What I say instead is quite simple: Indulge your curiosity, and don't be afraid to blunder every once in a while on the side of whimsy. There is a phrase that has come into vogue in recent years in academic circles, a strategy of education called the interdisciplinary approach. What this basically means in layman's terms is that a law professor should not feel constrained by the conventions of legal dogma from drawing, where appropriate, on the resources of the medical school or the business school to make a particular point, for instance, or not hesitate to factor the findings of some hot-shot government or economics professor into the equation. Indeed, many liberal arts colleges today allow undergraduates to design their own majors, drawing on the resources of all academic departments to create something that builds off their particular strengths and interests.

For the collector, there is wisdom in this philosophy. Just because you collect monographs documenting the history of American art doesn't mean you should pass up an opportunity to form a collection on the influence of photography on the medium, assuming good material is available and the price is right; the idea is to have fun, and if there are connections to be made along the way, so much the better. You might learn, for example, that in addition to being one of the outstanding American realist painters of the late nineteenth and early twentieth centuries, Thomas Eakins (1844–1916) was an enthusiastic pioneer in the use of photography. It is your job as the storyteller to link them together, to attach the dots on what otherwise might be regarded as a blank landscape. Who knows, you may at some point want an antique camera or two, something that brings a physical reality to your collection, and of course you won't stop there; before long you'll be wanting some vintage photographs.

One thing has a way of leading to another, and while that may be an awkward way to express a technique of collecting, so be it; like the concept of associative browsing nurtured at the London Library, I like the idea of enjoying what I call associative collecting. In 1985 I acquired a comprehensive collection of the works of Walker Percy (1916–1990) that included not only all of the physician-doctor's published works up to that time, but a wonderful variety of other materials, including signed copies of the memoir and poetry of William Alexander Percy (1885–1941), Percy's beloved "Uncle Will" and mentor, and numerous critical works. There was also a first edition copy of *A Confederacy of Dunces* (1980), the posthumously published comic novel that was published by Louisiana State University Press at the behest of Percy after the suicide of John Kennedy Toole, the author, and that went on to win a Pulitzer Prize, and a copy of the fall 1956 issue of *Partisan Review,* containing Percy's first piece of published fiction, the short story "The Man on the Train," and bearing his signature on the cover.

How I obtained this collection is worth noting; I had been pretty desperate to find a first edition copy of *The Moviegoer*, Percy's great novel about a young New Orleans stockbroker named Binx Bolling who views the world with the detached gaze of a Bourbon Street dandy and secretly yearns for a spiritual redemption that he cannot fully grasp. Let me say that there is a certain raw trenchancy to Percy's writing that touches me in a deeply personal way, and I regard him as one of the great literary voices of the twentieth century. He was at the front of my want list of authors that I wanted to acquire, and probably the one author among all others that I dearly wanted to interview for my newspaper columns, but was never able to arrange. We did meet once in 1982 in Washington, D.C., at a memorable function organized at the Smithsonian Institution by the Library of America to promote some new releases—Eudora Welty and C. Vann Woodward were there as well—but to my everlasting regret, I never managed to arrange a get-together with him. Keeping my fingers crossed all the same, I had meanwhile put the word out among my bookseller friends that Walker Percy was at the top of my list, and one day Joseph Dermont, a dealer from Onset, Massachusetts, now relocated in Rowland, Pennsylvania, and a principal provider in my early years of collecting, called and offered to sell me his own collection of Percy material that he had been building over a period of years. Knowing as I did how passionately Joe felt about Percy's work, I was deeply moved by the offer, especially since he said he was tendering it to someone he knew would care for the books with the same respect that he had.

We even worked out terms that enabled me to pay for the material over time, an agreement we repeated a couple of years later when he acquired for me a great sixteen-volume set of the works of Herman Melville, the standard edition published by Constable and Company Ltd., of London, in 1924, featuring the first appearance in print of *Billy Budd* and the *Poems*. These were not the kind of books I could possibly afford on a newspaperman's salary, and I would not be their custodian today if not for the care and interest one dealer took in helping a budding collector achieve a dream.

But the wonderful comprehensiveness of my Walker Percy collection—which continues growing to this day, incidentally, with the addition of the winter 2002 edition of *Double-Take* magazine, featuring a previously unpublished Percy essay on language, "Peirce and Semiotic"—is not the reason I mention it in the context of this chapter. My interest in Percy began, as I mentioned, with a desire to own a first edition of *The Moviegoer,* which had been published in 1961 in a very small first printing said to be no more than fifteen hundred copies, but winner the following year of the National Book Award, beating out such formidable rivals as Joseph Heller's *Catch-22,* John Updike's *Rabbit Run,* John Steinbeck's *Winter of Our Discontent,* and Bernard Malamud's *A New Life*. When it occurred to me just how strong the field for that prestigious prize was that year—and here we are today, more than forty years later, and each of these novels remains firmly entrenched in the American canon—I wondered if 1961 could be approached in the same way that the great critic Malcolm Cowley regarded other watershed years in American literature, most notably 1851, when Herman Melville's *Moby-Dick* and Nathaniel Hawthorne's *The House*

of the Seven Gables arrived full-blown into the world, followed within months by Harriet Beecher Stowe's *Uncle
Tom's Cabin* and all the tumult that work brought upon the
world. All sorts of possibilities develop from this kind of a
premise; you can begin collecting the productions of a particular year, you can consider the political, social, economic,
and cultural events of an era. If it was at a defining point in
your own lifetime—and 1961 was the year I graduated high
school, began college, graduated four years later, went off to
war a few years after that, and fell in love before the decade
had ended—then it can become very personal indeed. As I
say, one thing leads to another, and while associative collecting has the potential for being *thorough,* it does not necessarily have to be *complete.* In the jargon of the bibliophile,
completism is another matter entirely. Read on.

Of Thomas J. Wise (1859–1937), John Carter wrote that
the influential English bookman "seems to have been from
his earliest days a collector of quite uncommon foresight,
knowledge, shrewdness, perseverance and acquisitive skill,"
with particular strengths apparent in *taste* and *method,* two
words that crop up again and again in book collecting to the
point of tedium. Wise concentrated a good deal of his efforts
on contemporary writers, quite a departure from the norm
for the period, and he went so far as to acquire primary
material from the authors themselves or, in the case of Alger-
non Charles Swinburne, all that poet's surviving manuscripts
from his estate. "He not only acquired books from these
authors and their friends," Carter wrote, "but also made
himself an authority on their lives and works; and the fashion for collecting them was firmly cemented by the impressive series of bibliographies in which Wise set out, with a

wealth of detail quite new to such type of work, the complete roster of their literary productions."

Wise was what we would call a *completist,* a collector who seeks out every fragment produced by a chosen author. His zeal was such that he staked what otherwise would have been a sterling reputation on the forgery of one hundred "earlier" printings of works by his favorites, copies that he subsequently "discovered" in his supposed investigations, and then wrote about in his bibliographies, thereby giving them scholarly stature, and considerable monetary value on top of that. Wise's undoing came in 1934 when Carter, then a young bibliographer at the British Library, and a colleague, Graham Pollard, applied what were then pioneering scientific tests on the papers, fonts, and inks that had been used, to prove that the pamphlets were forgeries. They published their findings in *An Enquiry into the Nature of Certain Nineteenth-Century Pamphlets,* a devastating exposé of Wise's bibliographical misdemeanors, despite its rather tame title.

Wise never acknowledged his fabrications, but his reputation was shattered, and he died a broken man, the ultimate irony being that his forgeries today are exceedingly collectible in their own right. One of the finest collections of materials dealing with literary forgeries in the United States is at the University of Delaware, the gift of Dr. Frank W. Tober (1919–1995), a scientist with the DuPont Company whose interests were far-reaching. His collection includes the history of printing, the French Revolution, and ephemera, but his pride and joy were the four thousand books, pamphlets, and manuscripts from all periods that had one element in common—all dealt in one manner or other with forgeries or were actual forgeries themselves, an interest quickened by his own career as a research chemist. Considered the centerpiece of the collection—which was the subject of a well-attended exhibition at the University of Delaware in 1999—are fifty examples of the Thomas J. Wise forgeries, along with an archive of eighty-five autograph letters Wise wrote pertaining to bibliographical matters. I cite this case not so much to rehash the odd circumstances of the tale, which was quite sensational in book circles when it unfolded, but to point out the lengths to which some collectors will go to get everything a favored author has produced.

Especially pertinent here is that these were not forgeries in any conventional sense. Wise was not attempting to pass off fabricated work as coming from the pen of a favored author, and thus deceive the literary establishment in the way that William Henry Ireland tried in 1794 to demonstrate that a work of gibberish he cobbled together in his study was a newly found Shakespeare play with the unlikely title of *Vertigren and Rowena,* or the way that Clifford Irving bamboozled a good segment of the American publishing industry in 1972 with what he purported to be the "autobiography" of the billionaire Howard Hughes.

What Wise did instead was find some obscure compositions that actually had been written by such authors as Charles Dickens, George Eliot, Alfred Lord Tennyson, Rudyard Kipling, Robert Louis Stevenson, and the like and then, working in concert with Harry Buxton Forman (1842–1917), a master printer, create what he would then assert was an obscure, undocumented edition in which the writings had appeared in an earlier state. Remarkably, these hoaxes succeeded for upward of thirty years, and research into their legitimacy continued long after Wise's death. For our purposes, the larger point is that the target of Wise's machinations was not the great literary scholars of his day, because that sort of chicanery would have been uncovered quickly; his prey instead were unwitting book collectors of some means who felt driven to have "everything." One of his hapless victims was John Henry Wrenn, a Chicago financier whose collection of six thousand rare books, including a fairly complete run of forged pamphlets bought directly from Wise, were donated to the University of Texas at Austin in 1918, earning the dubious distinction of being the university's first rare-book collection. John Carter explained Wise's formula rather succinctly in an update to the *Enquiry* published in the *Atlantic* in 1945:

> So long as he was careful to print from the logical text; if the format and imprint were appropriate; if the hypothetical circumstances of publication and the position in its author's bibliography were plausible; and if he could then get his product on to the right shelves and into the right reference books, it was possible, as Wise proved in spite of mistakes, to get away with murder.

As generally understood, completism is synonymous with leaving no stone unturned in the quest to have it all. Insight and discretion have little bearing in the matter; if there is a fragment of juvenilia, for instance, that was published in the high school yearbook of a favored author, a completest is emboldened to own it. To help them along, detailed lists of writings are available for thousands of authors; in modern literature, arguably the most influential is *Ernest Hemingway: A Comprehensive Bibliography* (Princeton, NJ, 1967) by Audre

Hanneman, a Kansas City, Missouri, woman who spent the better part of twenty years compiling what Charles Scribner Jr. hailed in a foreword as a "task comparable to one of the fabled labors of Hercules." The gathering of such arcania as the size of the printings and the color of the cloth used on the bindings was just the beginning. Hanneman's designation of categories to identify different kinds of works by and about Hemingway has become standard in bibliographical circles and provides a kind of guidepost for people who have the will, the means—dare I say the patience and the fortitude—to be completists. When I stress, for instance, that as a collector of literary first editions I am only interested in acquiring A items, I mean the primary works as they have appeared for the first time between hard covers; I am selectively interested in B items for favored authors, and not at all interested in C, D, E, F, G, or H items. When I am using jargon like this among book people, most have a pretty good idea of what I am talking about. Briefly stated, the categories go like this:

A: Major works in books or pamphlets.

B: First appearance in book form of short stories, articles, dispatches, poems, as well as introductions to works of fiction and nonfiction.

C: All known work in newspapers and periodicals.

D: Published works in translation.

E: Anthologies containing the author's work.

F: Published facsimiles of manuscripts and letters.

G: Books and criticism written about the author.

H: Newspaper and periodical material written about the author.

To a far lesser degree, another form of completist is the person who collects everything on a certain list, be it every author who has ever won a Pulitzer Prize, a National Book Award, a Bancroft Prize, a Booker Prize, a Prix Goncourt, every science fiction writer who has won the Hugo Award or the Nebula Award, every crime writer to win an Edgar Allan Poe Award or a Silver Dagger Award, every book listed on the Modern Library 100 Best Works of Fiction and Nonfiction published in the twentieth century, that sort of thing. Then there is the Grolier Club List of 100 Best American Books, and the Grolier Club's List of 100 Books Famous in Medicine compiled by the late Dr. Haskell L. Norman, whose library of books important in science and medicine sold for $18.6 million at a Sotheby's auction in 1997. The book thief Stephen C. Blumberg stole books from 268 libraries in forty-five states, two Canadian provinces, and the District of Columbia over a thirty-year period, specializing for the most part in Americana, but with a soft spot for incunabula, gathering up more than a hundred fifteenth-century printed books in his travels, and determined to get every book listed on the Zamorano Club of Los Angeles list of eighty books central to the history of California. He began with the Zamorano Club's collection of its own books, housed at the time in the special collections unit of Claremont College. Unable to get a complete cycle there—only two complete sets were known, one at Yale University, the other in the home of a private collector, now deceased—Blumberg plotted ways to get the final prize he needed to finish off "his" run, a scheme that never went beyond the planning stage but drove him to distraction all the same and figured prominently at his trial in Des Moines, Iowa, in 1991.

Collectors who do their own primary research develop lists continually, lists that make perfectly good sense to them, and oftentimes serve an important scholarly function while they're at it. The variety of pursuits is as diverse as the human experience itself, and examples abound. Indeed, I come across them all the time, and whenever it happens, I think in amusement about those who say that there is nothing of substance left to collect anymore, that all the important material is gone. Certainly one of the towering examples of a person finding a neglected niche is the George Arents Collection at the New York Public Library, the most comprehensive assembly in the world of the history, literature, and lore of tobacco, several hundred thousand objects in twenty languages, the product of six decades of collecting by a former principal of the American Tobacco Company. On a more modest scale is the Jay Miller Aviation History Collection, the outgrowth of forty years of intensive private collecting by a former curator at the Humanities Research Center of the University of Texas, and since 1995 maintained by the Central Arkansas Library System in Little Rock, Arkansas. In addition to the six thousand books on flight history are fifty thousand journals, including complete runs of numerous aviation periodicals, and hundreds of operation manuals for aircraft that have not been in production for dozens of years. There also are broadsides, pamphlets, aeronautical charts, aviation art, technical reports, and 650 linear feet of unprocessed manuscript material, scrapbooks, and photographs, altogether an extraordinary archive now available to scholars and students. And then there is the culinary arts collection of the late Louis Szathmary, which was so vast it was distributed among numerous institutions, the rare books going to the University of Iowa, thousands of kitchen devices and other books to Johnson & Wales University in Providence, Rhode Island, a million menus to the University of Nevada, Las Vegas.

In 1997, a computer software engineer from Rochester, New York, named Michael J. Ciaraldi donated sixty thousand comic books, graphic novels, and assorted materials relating to popular art in American culture to Brown University, a collection that had been twenty-five years in the making, and was believed to be one of the largest archives of its kind anywhere. "It's not just superheroes, it's everything" was the ebullient response of Rosemary L. Cullen, the curator responsible for integrating the collection into the university's John Hay Library. "There's every sort of artwork, from really elegant styles to dripping guts to romantic sorts of things." As to the value of maintaining such an archive in one of America's premier Ivy League institutions, Cullen had this to say: "Comics aren't immediately thought of as a research tool, but they portray the ideas and attitudes of a particular time. There also are comics that focus on specific historical events, like Vietnam and Desert Storm."

For skeptics who think that perhaps Brown University might be putting a clever spin on what might otherwise be perceived as an oddball collection, consider the respectful coverage the *New York Times* gave in March 2002 to an exhibition mounted at the Sheldon Memorial Art Gallery at the University of Nebraska—ostensibly a "temple of high modernism"—called "Comics, Heroes and American Visual Culture," and featuring selected examples from a collection of original comicstrip art donated by Daniel F. Howard, a painter and former chairman of the art and art history department at the university. "Comic artists have developed dynamic and powerful aesthetic vocabularies that seize and sustain attention through the creative juxtaposition of words and images," read a sign at the entrance to the show. "This flies in the face of everything we've done before," Daniel A. Siedell, the museum curator, told the *Times*. "Our collection is changing. The tension is really there between popular and high art, and the challenge we're looking at now is how to integrate this into the collection we already have."

When I was signing books at an International League of Antiquarian Booksellers fair in San Francisco in 1996, I met a physician who ran an HIV clinic in the Bay Area who said he had begun a collection documenting the history and literature of AIDS, an absolutely fabulous undertaking, I felt instantly, which one day would make for an excellent research collection somewhere. For openers, the doctor said he was interested in works of fiction and poetry that had emerged in response to the deadly epidemic. *Plays Well with Others* (1997), a novel by Allan Gurganus, and Mark Doty's *My Alexandria* (1992), winner of a National Book Critics Circle Award, would be prime examples in this regard; even Saul Bellow's 2000 novel, *Ravelstein,* in which the central character, a famous Midwestern professor, is dying of the disease, probably would qualify. But he also was interested in articles published in professional journals that documented research into the continuing quest for a cure, and among the items he had gathered were materials that he had determined represented the first published uses of the word AIDS, an anagram for Acquired Immune Deficiency Syndrome. He also sought out works of nonfiction such as Randy Shiltes's *And the Band Played On* (1987) that have heightened social awareness of the virus and its consequences. There is no doubt that medical research centers throughout the world have libraries that teem with pertinent scientific articles in this field, but how many of them, I wonder, also have the works of fiction, poetry, and general nonfiction that give balance and texture to the human consequences of this twentieth-century nightmare? There will come a time, I am sure, when a collection like this will be in great demand.

For all the physician's determination, however, an effort like his can never be complete in any logical sense, as the sheer volume of material that has been produced—not to mention that which continues to be produced—is beyond the capabilities of any professional librarian with the means and the will to attempt it, let alone those of a private individual. So once again the collector defines what is important to the structure, and what the parameters ought to be. By determining the scope and the direction of what qualifies for inclusion, the collector remains in control of what is going on.

In this regard I think in particular of thirty-five books that I saw early in 2002 during a speaking visit to Marist College in Poughkeepsie, New York. In terms of content, these books had nothing in common; what made them remarkable—and what makes them a distinctive collection—are the fore-edge paintings that decorate the outer leaves of the volumes. Practiced sparingly today, fore-edge paintings were in vogue in Great Britain during the seventeenth and eighteenth centuries, and are quite beautiful to behold. What makes them remarkable is not so much the original paintings themselves, though some are elegantly done, but the clever way the images are made to appear when the pages of the books are fanned out, and concealed when squared up. The books in the James A. Cannavino Library were gathered by two benefactors of Marist College, George M. and Alice S. Gill, and though numbering just under three dozen, were believed to be the most significant collection of fore-edge paintings in private hands at the time they were turned over to the school in 1995. Because most books with paintings like this are done by hand, and because most of these unique items are unsigned and undocumented, a comprehensive bibliography is impossible; what the collector decides to collect, in other words, becomes the collection, not what some list asserts that it should be.

Another example of a totally individualized approach is the "oddities" collection assembled by Fred J. Board of Stamford, Connecticut. Amused by a reading of *Bookmen's Bedlam* (1955), Board contacted the author, Walter Hart Bluementhal, and arranged to purchase the books from his personal collection that had been described in it, a nutty assortment of volumes notable for their peculiarities—books shaped in the outline of states, books salvaged from sunken ships, books bound in human skin, books printed at sea. Using them as a core holding, Board expanded and enlarged on the theme, adding books shaped like circles, books printed on pasta, books held together by steel bolts, books that opened like accordions, books printed in white ink on purple paper, eccentric in every way, but not so bizarre as to discourage the Beinecke Rare Book and Manuscript Library at Yale University from mounting an exhibition featuring some of the weirdest examples. "The beauty about my specialty is that it's endless," Board told me. "There's no bibliography, there are hundreds of curious things in the world, and I'm the one who decides what is strange and unusual. I'm also the one who says when it's complete."

CHAPTER 6

THE BEAT GOES ON

As we have discussed, determining what a gathering of books *is* and what it *is not* is the true joy of a personal collection, the element that gives it an indelible mark. For years I had assumed that the prominent western Massachusetts bookseller Ken Lopez, a specialist in modern first editions, had put together two extraordinarily pertinent collections relating to the literature of the Vietnam War and the literature of Native Americans as a result of his personal experience and background. It turned out that I was wrong in both cases, yet for reasons that are illuminating just the same.

"I got interested in these areas not because of what I *was*, but because of what I *was not*," Lopez told me when I had asked him what branch of service he had served in during the war. "I was a protestor, and when my name went into the draft lottery in 1970, I went underground, and when I was underground I met a bunch of vets, guys who were just like me, but living under different circumstances, guys who had made different decisions. So the war, how it was perceived by novelists and poets and people who were there, became an obsession with me." After the war, Lopez worked as a book scout and began acquiring material for himself on Vietnam, and by the time he became a professional dealer in the mid-1970s, he had put together an impressive collection of several hundred works of literature and memoirs, all pertaining to the American misadventure in Southeast Asia. For his first catalog, devoted entirely to what he readily agrees was the event of his generation, Lopez asked the writer Robert Olen Butler, winner of a Pulitzer Prize in 1993 for *A Good Scent from a Strange Mountain,* a collection of stories dealing with the war, to write an introduction. By that time, Lopez had identified 750 titles as pertinent to the bibliography he had single-handedly compiled, and he established himself as the authority in the field. It wasn't long before universities were taking note of what he had assembled. "Once I pretty much had the collection complete, I broke it up into three distinct parts, and sold them to Colorado State University, La Salle University, and the University of Tulsa; then I assembled another collection that was comparable, and sold it to the University of Massachusetts Boston, which has a center for Vietnam studies." A similar dynamic developed in his assembly of a Native American Literature collection. "I grew up in the Bronx, I had never been on an Indian reservation in my life," Lopez said. "Here again, I was responding to something that I *wasn't,* yet something that engaged me in a very powerful way."

For Charles L. Blockson, the great collector of African-American books, pamphlets, prints, manuscripts, narratives, posters, photographs, sheet music, and broadsides, just the opposite kind of driving force was at work. Told when he was eight years old by a fourth grade teacher that "negroes have no history, they were born to serve white people," Blockson was determined from that point on to become, in his words, a "black bibliophile," a goal he achieved so triumphantly that the great assemblage of items he gathered now comprise a research collection at Temple University in Philadelphia that bears his name, and employs him as curator. And how did he begin his quest when he was just getting started as a child back in the late 1940s and early 1950s? Beginning at such places as Salvation Army and Goodwill stores, he singled out all items that he determined mentioned the words *black, Negro, African,* or *colored,* and took it from there. "They had books for ten cents each," he told me. "There were times when I buried books I wanted beneath others and waited until they had their half-price sales."

Aaron Lansky, meanwhile, was motivated to scour North America in search of anything at all printed in Yiddish for the simple reason that the materials were being thrown away and the language was in jeopardy of being lost through neglect and indifference. His quixotic mission, begun in 1980, resulted in the triumphant establishment of the National Yiddish Book Center in Amherst, Massachusetts, and the distribution of many thousands of books to colleges and universities on all five continents. The one rule he has imposed from the beginning of the quest—that no money be *paid* for any books—remains unchanged.

I think of examples like these when I hear people complain that there is nothing left to collect today, that all the good stuff is gone, to which I ask: Who says? All you have to do is look around and take stock of what is going on in the world to come up with worthwhile ideas. The heinous attack on the United States on September 11, 2001, presents a plethora of possibilities that could prove to be revealing windows into our turbulent times. As a modest start for my own edification, I set aside every copy of the *New York Times* from September 12 through September 25, 2001, fourteen days in which every edition featured a banner headline across page 1, not a record for the newspaper in wartime, I later learned from the newspaper's archivist—that would be a seemingly unsurpassable 141 consecutive issues, from December 21, 1944, through May 10, 1945, during World War II—but an extraordinary passage in recent American history nevertheless. The record for consecutive banner headlines in peacetime, I also learned from that telephone call—and I have saved all of them as well—is November 8 through November 27, 2000, twenty issues altogether, which followed the surreal process of deciding who would be the forty-third president of the United States. From a collecting standpoint, what these materials represent is a good beginning, nothing more. But the possibilities are in place for a multitude of options. Fire fighting has always been a popular field for collectors, and to no one's great surprise, it is much more popular now, with the element of heroism in all its manifestations taking on a deeper texture, which raises yet another possibility, a gathering of books that considers the ways in which uncommon courage has been treated in children's literature over the years, and how it is being handled now.

I have a number of books published *since* 9/11—but *before* New Year's Day 2002—that have become valued additions to my library, and they came to me as review copies that I noticed in a holiday roundup I do every year for the syndicate of newspapers that take my literary features. One of the most spectacular efforts—indeed, it was my pick book of the year— was *Manhattan Unfurled,* a sweeping panorama of the city that never sleeps that stretches open accordion-style to a full twenty-two feet, East Side to West Side, a visual tour de force proving yet again how a book can be an artifact with a life quite apart from its text. Because the architect-illustrator Matteo Pericoli spent more than two years executing the elegant pen-and-ink drawings, the Twin Towers still stand proudly in his rendering. Another book I like just as much is *Celluloid Skyline: New York and the Movies,* by James Sanders, an architect-scriptwriter who examined the "actual" city of everyday life, and the "mythic" representation of it on film; this effort, too, was years in the making, and the decision to publish on schedule was explained in an author's note as a hopeful attempt that "may in some way help to further an understanding of why the New York skyline—in both image and reality—has had such profound and personal meaning for people around the world." Will these books be collectible? The only answer that matters in a case like this is mine, and I say yes, they will be, because it's my collection, and I decide what comes in, and what doesn't.

The idea that a person must acquire every state of every work produced by an important author remains a valid goal, certainly, and is by no means a superannuated doctrine, but as these examples suggest, the times have changed all the same. There was an era when books were treasured as much for their content as for their scarcity, a factor that still applies in many instances, but one that has been pushed out on the margins with the muscular arrival of computers. Today, information is available in staggering abundance on the Internet, by no means all of it, but in sufficient magnitude to make ownership of hard copies less a need for content than a desire to own original artifacts. Sir Isaac Newton, Charles Darwin, Benjamin Franklin, and Francis Parkman built libraries that were deemed magnificent in their time, but the driving motivation for them was to gratify a thirst for knowledge. Two of the most prominent expatriate booksellers working abroad in the mid-nineteenth century, Obadiah Rich and Henry Stevens, specialized in assembling research materials for such prominent American historians as Washington Irving, William Prescott, and George Bancroft. When Thomas Jefferson of Virginia confided to his friend John Adams in Massachusetts that he was unable to live without books, or when the colonial polymath James Logan was confessing plaintively to a London dealer three thousand miles from his home in Philadelphia that books were his "disease," the message in each case was clear; what these men of keen intellect were desperate to obtain were works of consuming interest that could be accessed nowhere else and, once acquired, became treasured possessions. It is worth recalling that there were no libraries of distinction during the time of the American colonies, or in the early years of the republic for that matter, which is why the great libraries of such luminaries as William Byrd and Thomas Jefferson of Virginia, and George Ticknor and William Prescott of Massachusetts, were gathered by people who craved the knowledge that books contained, knowledge that was not available to them elsewhere. The paucity of books in the United States during the early nineteenth century prompted John Quincy Adams to remark that any institution that could acquire just half of the titles cited by Edward Gibbon in his *Decline and Fall of the Roman Empire* would have a formidable library.

If Edgar Allen Poe's name had been printed anywhere in his anonymously published first book, then undoubtedly more copies of *Tamerlane and Other Poems* would have survived to the present day. Indeed, it is a matter of no small chagrin to the librarians at the Boston Athenæum that they do not have a copy of the work, since the private library had been around for five years when it appeared in 1812, and one may well have passed through the collections, given the fact that the publisher of the book was a member of the library and might have sent along a review copy of the work. As it is, only eleven copies of what is often referred to as the "black orchid" of American literature are known, most of them in institutional collections. The most recent unrecorded copy to come to light made headlines in the late 1980s when it was disclosed that a commercial fisherman who had been sifting through some old agricultural tracts in a New Hampshire antiques barn noticed an old volume buried in the bottom of the carton. Something about the item—"written by a Bostonian," is all it said on the title page to identify the author—captured his attention, so he bought it for $15, got a professional to take a look, then consigned it to Sotheby's in New York for sale, where it brought $198,000 at auction in 1989. That same year, even more spectacular headlines were generated when it was reported that a person buying a dull old painting at a flea market in Adamstown, Pennsylvania, supposedly because he liked the decrepit frame, was pleasantly surprised to discover a first issue copy of the Declaration of Independence folded and hidden behind the canvas; it brought in $2.5 million at auction, even though the neat story of how the anonymous buyer found the "famous $4 frame" was never explained to everyone's full satisfaction. That very same copy of the Declaration of Independence, incidentally, was sold by Sotheby's on June 29, 2000, in an on-line auction, bringing in a whopping $8.14 million, but I digress; for our purposes, what is noteworthy about such stories is that these kinds of discoveries do happen, and they happen all the time, though not always with the same dramatic results, and with far less fanfare.

My own discovery of Emily Dickinson's exceedingly scarce first book of poems was far less spectacular, but no less exciting for me. I found it in remarkably good condition at a yard sale during a drive through northern Worcester County one Saturday afternoon in the early 1980s, stacked upright in a cardboard box with nineteen other volumes priced at fifteen dollars per title, ten dollars each if I took them all, a concession I happily accepted. How the affable woman offering these books arrived at this arbitrary price I have no clue, since eighteen of the twenty would have been overpriced at two dollars each had I encountered them at a library discard sale, where, in fact, the excess finally went, with my compliments; the twentieth book in the box, though by no means as exciting as the Emily Dickinson, turned out to be a prize all the same, *Rural Poems* by William Barnes, published in Boston in 1869 by Roberts Brothers. Contemporary readers can be forgiven if the name of the poet does not strike a resonant chord, since it is not the stylized verses that make this small volume—a *duodecimo,* in bookseller's jargon—such a welcome addition to my shelves, although the leather binding, gold stamped pictorial cloth, and elegant marbling on the pastedowns are quite attractive; it is the interior illustrations, specifically six of them by the American artist Winslow Homer, that elevates its desirability above the commonplace. Best known for his magisterial oil paintings, watercolors, and illustrations for *Harpers Weekly* during the mid-1800s, Homer did a number of wood engravings for books early in his career, with all of the documented examples itemized by Gordon Hendricks in a checklist of published graphics included in his monograph, *The Life and Work of Winslow Homer* (1979), an indispensable reference. I can't say I've committed all of these titles to memory, though I do know most of them—which is why I now own a good number of them as well—and I know enough to look for telltale evidence of his work whenever I pick up a late-nineteenth-century book published in Boston that features wood engravings. A collector who knows something about book illustration—one who knows, for instance, that these first appearance engravings were all pulled from the original woodblocks, which were then smoothed over and used again for other pictures—has an advantage over many dealers interested only in the names of the authors, an advantage that will pay rich dividends. It is partly for this reason that I regard a small magnifying glass as essential equipment to carry along with me on my booking expeditions, the better to determine whether or not a beautiful illustration I know nothing about is, let's say, a lithograph, which would make it quite desirable, or merely a reproduction printed on an offset press, which would render it far less so. (If it's the latter, the patterns will show up under magnification as a matrix of small dots; the former will reveal itself as multiple layers of ink.)

But to get back to my acquiring those twenty books in a cardboard box, the question remains, since I knew I was onto something immediately, of whether or not I took advantage of this kindly woman, sensing, as I did, that I was getting a book, in the instance of the Dickinson, that now commands a price as high as five thousand dollars. Had I tried to "beat" her down on the price, then the answer would most definitely be yes, but I paid what she asked. I even splurged and took eighteen worthless books off her hands for the privilege of getting the two *finds* that I knew were there waiting to be rescued from what for all intents and purposes was a scrap heap. The long and short of the matter is that the woman was delighted with the deal, and I was as well—end of story— though that apparent outcome did not stop one acquaintance of mine, a former Trappist monk, from quipping, "If you go to hell, that will be the reason."

There are people who regard the owning of multiple copies of the same book as a form of heterodoxy, especially when the books in question happen to be in comparable condition. We have already discussed the concept of buying copies of the same book with the idea of "moving up" in quality; that is a different matter entirely. But prevailing wisdom says basically, listen, don't be a hog, let someone else have a whack at it. There is merit to that argument, and I subscribe to it for the most part, but please don't tell me I should stop looking for more copies of Celia Thaxter's *An Island Garden* with exquisite lithographic illustrations by the great American impressionist artist Childe Hassam, and contained in an exquisite binding designed by Sarah Wyman Whitman, since I already have four, because I won't listen. I found my copies years ago, when very few dealers knew much about the book beyond the obvious fact that it is gorgeous, arguably the most beautiful nineteenth-century book produced in the United States. What pleases me beyond words—and it has happened twice, at the Museum of Fine Arts in Boston, and again at the Yale University Art Gallery in New Haven—is to see a museum exhibition of Hassam's paintings or Whitman's bindings, and the copy of *Island Garden* on display nearby has been borrowed from another collection, and is clearly inferior to at least two of mine.

How come I was buying these books up twenty years ago for what today would be regarded as pocket money, and hardly anybody else was interested? The truth is that I am not all that prescient, but I have a friend, an art dealer, who excels as a master picker at the Brimfield Fair, the nation's largest flea market, held three times a year outside Sturbridge, Massachusetts, fifty miles west of Boston, who told me about the book when copies were still "out there" and available at reasonable prices. This is yet another example of the benefits of hanging around with people who have something to teach you; Brian Higgins of West Brookfield, Massachusetts, a talented pastel artist in his own right, has counseled me in the nuances of book illustration, and what are known as *livres d'artistes*. In return, I have shared with him what I know about book hunting, a solid case of synergy if ever there was one, a circumstance that proves mutually helpful whenever we go to book fairs and flea markets together. After he showed me his copy of *Island Garden,* with its magnificent chromolithographs by Hassam, I alerted all of my sources in the book trade to be on the lookout for copies. It certainly was not an unknown book, if you know where to look for information. The *Bibliography of American Literature* calls *An Island Garden* "one of the most elaborate pieces of bookmaking" of its time, and notes that just 1,019 first issue copies were printed, in March 1894, just a few months before Thaxter's death at the age of fifty-nine.

I became such a fan that I started badgering the people I knew at Houghton Mifflin through my work as a literary editor about the importance of a book they had published a century earlier, and these efforts finally paid off in 1988 with publication of a gorgeous facsimile edition, including a superb introductory essay by the respected horticultural writer Allen Lacy. What I found mildly amusing was the fact that Houghton Mifflin did not have a copy of the original book in its archives, and had to buy one on the antiquarian market before an exact copy could be made. There was even some talk for a while about using one of mine for the job, which I would have allowed with great reluctance, if pressed, but was relieved all the same when they found their own, since disbinding—or guillotining, as the process is known—would have been required to make a faithful facsimile. When that reprint sold out in 2001, Houghton Mifflin went back to press with another edition, this one with an appreciative introduction by the children's book illustrator from Vermont, Tasha Tudor.

In their comments, both Lacy and Tudor pointed out how Thaxter had been a poet of some renown during her lifetime, and how she is known today mainly for the single work of lyrical prose she wrote about her offshore garden of hollyhocks, poppies, scarlet flax, and the like. Thaxter lived during the spring and summer on Appledore on the Isles of Shoals, a group of rocky outcroppings about ten miles off the coast of New Hampshire, a ninety-eight-acre dot in the Gulf of Maine where her father had been a lighthouse keeper when she was growing up, and where she, in later years, maintained a kind of salon frequented by many artists, musicians, and literary figures of the period. Her great pride and joy was a brilliantly conceived garden, notable for the fact that it was maintained strictly for its beauty, not function, quite a departure in the nineteenth century, when agriculture was pursued principally as a means of producing food. Her tribute to the garden was immortalized in images by Childe Hassam (1859–1935), the great American Impressionist artist who spent many summers on Appledore, producing hundreds of paintings that are regarded as among his very best. An exhibition mounted by Yale University in 1990, *An Island Garden Revisited,* paid tribute to the work he produced there. The eleven chromolithographs made from the paintings for Thaxter's prose-tribute to her garden are said to have been made from as many as thirty stones, an extraordinarily costly and exacting process, and were inserted, or *tipped in,* in each volume separately. The binding, designed by the notable stained-glass designer, watercolorist, and bookmaker Sarah Wyman Whitman, features a graceful line of poppies stamped in gold on green cloth, though a few known as the "albino" variation—and I have one—were produced on white cloth.

As wonderful as this book is, and as wonderful as the Emily Dickinson volume may be, there is a larger point to this pair of book-hunting anecdotes. I acquired the Dickinson by happenstance, though serendipity is probably the more accurate word, while the Thaxters have come my way through determined pursuit. Both titles, in their own way, have become part of a small collection I have that is distinctive for the fact that they represent the elements of a story that appeals to me as a person who writes about books and authors, a linkage that never would have occurred to me had

I not given a great deal of thought, and done a good amount of research into the lives and the writing of these two women, both native New Englanders, both poets from the same era, and both dealing with a form of seclusion, but from entirely different perspectives.

Dickinson (1830–1886) lived in self-imposed isolation, writing largely for herself, allowing just seven poems to be published in her lifetime, five of them in the Springfield *Republican,* and two anonymously in the *Atlantic* through the intervention of the writer and abolitionist Thomas Wentworth Higginson, who advised her not to publish her work. It should be noted that Higginson's evaluation of Walt Whitman followed the conservative conventions of the time as well: "It is no discredit to Walt Whitman that he wrote *Leaves of Grass,* only that he did not burn it afterwards," he wrote of the *other* great American poet of the nineteenth century. As for Dickinson, only in death would she emerge as an artist of consequence—at which point Higginson pulled something of an about-face, and served as coeditor of the first two volumes of her posthumously released work. The years that have passed have brought stature and recognition that is without parallel for an American female poet of any period.

With Celia Laighton Thaxter (1835–1894), the situation was reversed. Though she lived much of her life a choppy boat ride ten miles east of Portsmouth on Appledore, she craved the intellectual stimulation that came from mixing among artistic people, and invited them to escape the summer heat of the cities by enjoying the cool Atlantic breezes that the accommodations she could offer made possible. Her poetry—pleasing rhymed concoctions that appealed to the sensibilities of the day—were published in numerous collections, a number of them elegant books that I also have sought out, and have been able to find through several dealers. By today's standards, Thaxter, who appeared in various popular magazine advertisements endorsing such commodities as typewriters and cigars, would be judged a celebrity. Charming little confections that they were, her poems are rarely anthologized and remain mostly forgotten, her name perpetuated largely by the passionate paean she wrote in tribute to her flowers, and the great good fortune she managed in persuading the artist Childe Hassam to produce some magnificent paintings to illustrate them. Another item I acquired—this one came to me through a bookseller's catalog, and at a surprisingly reasonable price—is one of the few books I own that qualifies as a unique artistic artifact. It is a copy of *The Cruise of the Mystery and Other Poems* by Celia Thaxter, a nondescript paperback published in 1886 by Houghton Mifflin. It is inscribed in green ink: "Harry Fenn from Celia Thaxter, July 1887," and bears the signatures of a few other subsequent owners; but these marks of prior ownership aren't what make it special. The person to whom the book is inscribed, Harry Fenn (1845–1911), was a prominent book illustrator of the nineteenth century; his work was widely reproduced and tremendously respected. Among his more notable efforts were the engravings he executed for William Cullen Bryant's *Picturesque America* (1872), which was proclaimed in its time by the art historian W. J. Linton to be "the most important book of landscapes that has appeared in this country." On successive pages of my copy of Celia Thaxter's volume of poetry, Fenn has painted in a series of watercolors, some of seaweed, others of mussels and driftwood; there is a fantastic scene of a sloop under full sail with a setting sun on the horizon, yet another with a seaside cliff in profile. All of these paintings are signed or initialed with Fenn's distinctive monogram, one of them including a notation in his hand, "Isles of Shoals, July 30th, '87," which would make it a full seven years *before* Childe Hassam's interpretations of Celia's beloved island garden appeared in print. So the question arises, did Celia invite Harry Fenn to Appledore with the hope that he might give visual energy to the verses she had written about the enduring majesty of her rocky domain? And tiring of an illustrated edition that never appeared in print, did she then turn her attention to Childe Hassam? A pleasant question for me to ponder as I continue to consider the "story line" of two very appealing collections. But there was more to come

Having become a Celia Thaxter admirer by way of a book that is outstanding for its art, and eager to put what I had learned about illustration to good use, I expanded my interest to take in every book illustrated by Childe Hassam and Harry Fenn, and from there I moved into locating books with illustrations by Winslow Homer and Frederic Remington, touching lightly along the way on the magazine and periodical engravings of Homer and Thomas Nast. This is just a sideline, mind you, and not a serious collection by any means, but it is the narratives I like most of all, and the objects that I have gathered around them that add the depth.

For Ronald Smeltzer, an electrical engineer with a doctorate from Northwestern University and now retired, a fascination for collecting old scientific instruments led seamlessly to the gathering of many pertinent books that describe and explain their use. "The first thing I obtained was a big brass microscope made in the nineteenth century in London by

Smith & Beck," Smeltzer told me. "Based on the inscription on the brass, it was presumably carried to the Crimean War, where, I have documented, the owner, Sir William Aiken, met Florence Nightingale. It was through her influence that Aiken got his first job after the war with the British government. Anyway, once I had that, I started buying books about the microscope, and that has led to everything else. It is fair to say that the collection began with artifacts, but now I'm only buying books, because artifacts take up a lot more space than books."

Still, what Smeltzer has gathered around him in his Princeton, New Jersey, home is impressive all the same, and everything is functional. Of particular note is a reflecting telescope made in England in 1767 by George Adams, "one of the few surviving examples with the original box containing an Adams trade card, one of only about a half-dozen still known, pasted inside." Smeltzer has gathered various eighteenth-century books written by Adams on the subject of this instrument. Another curiosity—Smeltzer calls it "a little radioactive toy from around 1900"—is a spinthariscope first made by Sir William Crookes, a contraption that "you look inside to see flashes of light as alpha particles hit a screen," the first method devised to count radioactive particles.

"I also have a six-prism spectroscope made by Browning, the most famous maker of these instruments, that is at the heart of a very nice collection I have on spectroscopy, a discipline in which you look at the color of light given off by various objects. An appealing aspect of this collection is that because we are talking about the spectrum, very often the books will have beautiful color plates. Another major collection I have is what I call Physics Since Newton. I do not have a *Principia* [1687], but I do have a number of books spawned by the rise of Newtonian physics. The key point about the rise of Newtonian physics was the emphasis on experimentation. The essence of Descartes's physics, on the other hand, was that Descartes never imagined how the world worked; he didn't worry about proving things. He thought a person's mind could develop a world picture about the way things happen, and he was wrong. One of Newton's many contributions was the premise that a theory had to be proven by experimentation. Eventually, experiment and theory have to agree, and this is the thrust of another collection I have developed, books on experimental physics that were published roughly from 1700 onward. Most of these books were published by people who gave lectures about physics and wrote them up in books that included beautiful illustrations of the equipment."

Smeltzer estimates there are something on the order of three thousand books in his collection, all built around a core of a dozen scientific instruments. "They're always on display, and not in storage," he emphasized. "I'm not interested in collecting things that I have to keep in a warehouse. They have to be nearby. It's the pleasure of seeing them, touching them, even using them. Occasionally I will set up some of the famous nineteenth-century experiments with the spectroscope, or I'll use the microscope to look at something." The book Smeltzer regards as the "most remarkable" in his collection is *Declaration de l'usage du graphometre* (Paris, 1597), by Philippe Danfrie, which describes the use of a French surveying instrument that was popular well into the eighteenth century. "My copy is bound in contemporary limp vellum, has gorgeous illustrations, and the text is printed with the civilité font, which emulates French handwriting of the period."

Although there is a decided antiquarian flavor to what he collects, Smeltzer does maintain what he regards as "one great twentieth-century modern physics collection" that begins in 1895 with the discovery in Germany of X rays by Conrad Roentgen and continues through the mid-1950s. "I have quite a few things dealing with the Manhattan Project and the development of the atomic bomb, and a good number of books that came immediately afterward to explain atomic energy to the layman."

Needless to say, every collection Smeltzer undertakes is grounded in detailed research. "Although I do have a number of high-spots, these are all in-depth collections. I'm glad to show them and explain their relevance, and there are times when I have to ease people out of the house at midnight: they're having too much fun and don't know when to leave. I maintain an excellent reference library, and I have research privileges at Princeton University, where I am active with the Friends of the Library." Because he knows more often than not exactly what he is looking for, Smeltzer has made good use of the Internet. "Generally I buy from established booksellers, and I use their individual websites, but I also have had very good success using addall.com as a global search engine."

As this example makes clear, the very best collectors make use of everything they have learned, they apply every skill they have mastered, they use every technique at their disposal. It is easy to say that somebody is a *completist* or an *author collector,* and that getting a full shelf of a favored writer's published works is the ultimate goal of the quest,

which may be all well and good. But for some collectors, that
is just the beginning of the exercise. I think in this context of
Daniel Posnansky, a native of the Bronx, now in his early six-
ties who has lived in the Boston area for the better part of
four decades. At one time vice president of Emerson College
and a longtime administrator at Harvard University, Posnansky has been collecting Arthur Conan Doyle (1859–1930)
since he was a teenager, and is a member of the Baker Street
Irregulars, the crème de la crème of Sherlock Holmes organizations, founded in 1934 by Christopher Morley (1890–
1957), the author of several entertaining books about books,
and a longtime editor of the *Saturday Review of Literature*.
The BSI, as the members refer to themselves, are as intense a
bunch of zealots as I have ever had the pleasure of meeting;
their charter requires all prospective members to be conversant with the "sacred writings" of Doyle, and to pass an examination demonstrating their knowledge of their contents. The
bylaws call for an annual meeting every January 6—Sherlock
Holmes was born on that day in 1884—an event highlighted
by the giving of a toast to the "canonical" works, "after
which the members shall drink at will," with rounds to be
bought successively by those failing to answer questions pertaining to the "sacred writings" posed by other members.
For pure fanaticism, these people are in a class among themselves, and the more eccentric they are in pursuit of all matters Sherlockian, the higher the esteem they enjoy among
their peers. Posnansky is also an officer in the Speckled Band
of Boston, a scion society of the Baker Street Irregulars, and
founder of another Holmes offshoot fellowship, the Friends
of Irene Adler at Harvard University, and one of the first to
admit women. This group is named for the heroine of the

story "A Scandal in Bohemia," the only instance in which a woman gets the better of Holmes.

"I don't think of myself as a completist, although I certainly have many thousands of Doyle things," Posnansky told me in one of many conversations we have had over the fifteen years I have known him. "I am what you might call an elitist. I like to buy things that are one of a kind, things that are so unusual that they take a lifetime to find. You might hear of such things when you are a little kid, and then you spend decades trying to locate them. Some of these items I am just finding now, and they are the things I love most of all. But to qualify for this elitist category, there has to be something about the item that is vitally important; it can't *just* be unique."

Posnansky estimates he has about ten thousand volumes and "assorted materials" pertaining to Arthur Conan Doyle and his great literary creation, the detective Sherlock Holmes, including a number of postcards going back a hundred years, some pieces of sheet music, and two hundred letters written by the master himself. "Many thousands of the books I have are piracies, which is a fascinating exercise unto itself, since so much of Doyle's work was stolen and used without his permission at the turn of the century, and it drove him nuts. I probably have the world's largest collection of Sherlock Holmes piracies, and they're mostly from the United States, since the copyright convention did not take hold until well into the twentieth century. I have identified something on the order of one hundred pirating publishers, most of whom were in New York, but some were in Chicago. I have had a lot of exhibitions featuring this material from my collection."

Indeed, the "elitist" part of Posnansky's Doyle collection

"is the cornerstone" of his "pirate collection." By far his most prized piracy is a book bearing an 1894 inscription from Doyle to the Chicago poet and bibliophile, Eugene Field. "The book itself is nothing, worth perhaps ten dollars without the inscription," Posnansky said. But inside, where Doyle has noted that this particular copy of *Sign of the Four* is a piracy, has been written the following quatrain:

> *This bloody pirate stole my sloop*
> *And holds her in his wicked ward.*
> *Lord send that walking on my poop*
> *I see him kick at my main-yard.*

The final word, mainyard, is a reference to the boom on a sailing ship where criminals were hanged at sea. Not content with just an inscription in words, Doyle also scribbled in a noose around the name of the publisher, United States Book Company, and drew in a skull and crossbones. "This is a very famous book, it has been well documented in a number of studies, and I spent thirty years tracking it down before I was finally able to buy it. What makes it really special is that this is the only occasion in which Doyle is known to have expressed in a book inscription how he felt about all the piracies of his work. He wrote a lot of letters about piracy, but this is the only documented instance of where he made his feelings known in the copy of a pirated book. And the thing that makes it really beautiful is that it is written in one of the most egregious examples of piracies you can find of his work."

Other "elite" items in Posnansky's collection include a letter from Franklin D. Roosevelt dated March 19, 1945, and written on White House stationery, to Edgar Smith, then the head of the Baker Street Irregulars, addressing him as "Buttons," which was Smith's BSI pen name. "Everyone who comes into the BSI gets an investiture associated with the canon, and the content of this letter is proof positive that FDR was a member, something we have been unable to document otherwise. We still don't know what Roosevelt's investiture was—my sense, in fact, is that he didn't have one, the reason being is that he was already invested with the title of President of the United States—the club has never been much at keeping good records, I am embarrassed to say." Posnansky has another letter to Smith, also on White House stationery, from Harry Truman, dated December 15, 1945, some four months after he had ordered the atomic bombing of Japan. Truman thanked the BSI for offering *him* honorary membership, and offered a telling postscript: "I commend your good sense in seeking escape from this troubled world into the happiest and calmer world of Baker Street. I had read all of the Holmes novels before I was twelve years old and I would do it again if I had the time."

Posnansky had other items to show me, most triumphantly a bookseller's "dummy" copy of the first American edition of *The Hound of the Baskervilles,* which he acquired in 1990 from a dealer who had just paid twenty-five cents for it, and for which Posnansky, in turn, "happily paid" five thousand dollars. Called a dummy because it contains mostly blank pages, the volume—used as a traveling book salesman's sample in the early years of the twentieth century—contains a copyright page that is identical to what must have appeared in the very first issue of the book, but had never been seen, since only about a hundred were said to have been produced before changes were ordered by the printer.

Posnansky explained: "This was so critical for me, because it was proof positive of something that had been rumored about the first American printing of this book, but had never been proved, that this most famous Holmes book of all was issued in about a hundred copies without the name of the British publisher on the copyright page. I knew all about this because it had been written up in 1962 by a Doyle scholar who admitted that he had never seen a copy. Now I had proof, but it was only in a bookseller's dummy. So now let's fast-forward four or five years. By happenstance I learn of an auction about to take place—I'd rather not say, for reasons you will understand in a moment, exactly where—and I see that there is a *Hound of the Baskervilles,* described as the dummy, listed for sale. I call the auctioneer immediately and I ask him to describe what he has. He thinks he has the dummy, but it is clear to me that what he has is the *actual* book, with the verso of the title page that matches that of the dummy. So I arrange to have a friend go to the auction and bid for me. I instruct this person that I will pay up to $30,000 for the book, it is that crucial an object; the person calls back and says I got it for $282. I have to say this is one of the greatest items in my collection, and is the perfect example of what I call the elitist approach. It is so important—and I am the only person in the world who has it. Can it possibly get any better than that?"

When I hear stories like this, I think of a comment offered by William Harris Arnold in a 1930 treatise on book collecting: "When a man says, 'Luck came my way,' he doesn't mean exactly that. He means that he really knows where good opportunities are likely to be found; and he takes his stand right there and waits patiently, as the intelligent hunter for his big game." In 1937, the author, collector, and bibliographer Michael Sadleir offered a similar sentiment in words that I liked so much, I used them as an epigraph for *A Gentle Madness*: "In nature the bird who gets up earliest catches the most worms, but in book-collecting the prizes fall to birds who know worms when they see them."

CHAPTER 7

EARNING YOUR METTLE

At every opportunity I get, I like to hammer home my considered belief that the best collectors are the people who *know* their subjects as well or better than anyone else, hardly an earth-shattering revelation, but one that always seems to get short shrift in every guide I have ever read on the pastime. You can devour all the primers in the world for advice on such fundamental concepts as taste and technique, but unless you are willing to do your homework—to become conversant with the literature in your chosen field, to learn the rudiments of bibliography, to *read,* for goodness sake—you are doomed to mediocrity. It seems absurd to have to say something so elemental as that, but we are talking about *book* collecting here, not the hoarding of seashells, refrigerator magnets, whirligigs, bottle caps, or Barbie dolls, and sometimes that basic reality gets lost in the mist of the rhetoric.

The larger point to be made is that to excel in this endeavor, you have to be willing to bring something to the table, and by that I do not mean a stack of chips to underwrite your action as a player, I mean your imagination, your intelligence, your eagerness to explore and to learn, your willingness to improvise and to innovate in areas others might consider a waste of precious time. Expressed in a less delicate way, I defer to a no-nonsense assessment offered in 1982 by Grant Uden, a British librarian and writer of some renown. "If someone asks me 'What shall I collect?' I am tempted to reply 'If you have to ask the question—nothing'; for this vague approach seems to me to be prompted by unsound motives," he wrote in a learned monograph, *Understanding Book-Collecting*. Instead of advising people *what* they should collect—"who am I to decide for you your whims and fancies, your unpredictable likings and loves"—Uden focused instead on some aspects of the *how,* offering up an erudite introduction to a number of technical matters that he felt should be mastered by the curious before setting out for the bookstalls in pursuit of buried treasure. "Knowledge of facts is as fundamental in book collecting as in mathematics," Winslow L. Webber wrote in a 1937 "bio-bibliography for collectors" titled *Books About Books*. "In both instances, one is either right or wrong."

If it is true, as John Fleming stressed, that *condition, condition, condition* are the three most important qualities to look for in a rare book, then it also is true that *research, research, research* are the prime elements that sharpen the field skills of the inveterate book hunter. In chapter 4, Katharine Kyes Leab confided that before she will sell a novice collector a copy of *American Book Prices Current*, the annual record of auction sales she has prepared since 1972—and copies are sold principally through Dan and Kathy Leab's company, not in bookstores—she recommends that some preliminary visits to a local library be made before a final decision on making the purchase is reached. "People have to know what things *are* before they can know what they are *worth,*" she told me with a slight hint of exasperation. "And, if you're going to collect successfully, you must be passionately interested in the subject you are collecting. An investment banker who wanted to collect books once approached me, saying, 'I'm told bird books are good.' It is true that bird books are pricey and easily convertible to cash, but I asked, 'Do you like birds? Are you a birdwatcher?' 'No,' he said, 'but I'm told they're a good thing to collect.' I then inquired, 'What do you *like*?' It turned out that he liked the writings of the physicist Werner Heisenberg, quantum mechanics, parallel universes, black holes, that sort of stuff. So I asked him, 'Why don't you collect *that*?' And with utter incredulity, he said, '*Could I?*' As though it might not be *possible,* or even worse, *acceptable.*"

In *Patience & Fortitude,* I included a chapter I called "Madness Redux" as a kind of appreciative bow to *A Gentle Madness,* the book that got me deeply involved in the world of the bibliophile. While that chapter recalled the spirit of its predecessor, there was additional motivation beyond mere sentiment to include it, as I take pains to point out in the talks I give to various bibliophilic societies around the country. What I chose to do with that chapter, I like to say, was explore the activities of six collectors who would have been very much at home in *A Gentle Madness*—if only I had known about them at the time I was writing the book. Beyond that cute remark, however, lies a much larger reality that argued for their inclusion, and it involves preparation for the task at hand. The six collectors profiled in "Madness Redux"—Abel Berland, Diana Korzenik, Carol Fitzgerald, Jay Fliegelman, Rolland Comstock, and Minor Myers Jr.—may have taken decidedly different approaches to fulfilling their separate passions, but before any of them could reach their goals, they had to become experts in their fields. The word *scholar* is not inappropriate in this instance, indeed it is pretty much on the mark, but I am not emphasizing the kind of inquiry that requires a tenured position in a university to conduct, although in some instances, without question, the writing of a book or monograph may be the ultimate goal. What I am talking about instead is the kind of research that is within the reach of anyone who has the will to undertake it. The materials the six people in "Madness Redux" went after may have ranged in price from several dollars spent at flea markets for ephemeral items to six figures bid in the galleries of the world's most elegant auction houses, but in every instance, there was an informed purpose at work, a larger goal to achieve, and that was to make sense of *something* through a collection of books.

In the case of Abel Berland, a retired Chicago real estate developer who had collected exquisite copies of Western literature over four decades, the commitment involved tireless reading in his *study* as a prelude to the late-night privilege of spending time alone with the books he had gathered in his *library*. Following a more traditional path of scholarly inquiry—and operating, it must be emphasized, with far more modest means at her disposal—Diana Korzenik, an art professor in Massachusetts, single-handedly created a genre of study through her incessant excursions in the New England countryside seeking out at flea markets and yard sales the largely ephemeral items she needed to document art instruction in American public schools during the nineteenth century. Rarely spending more than ten or twenty dollars for the materials she found, Korzenik formed an archive of material that is now installed as a research collection of distinction at the Huntington Library in California, one that bears her name as both innovator and donor.

For Carol Fitzgerald of Fort Lauderdale, Florida, the subject of choice was the Rivers of America series of books published in the United States between 1936 and 1964, and a monumental quest on her part to locate and acquire not only examples of every edition and issue of the thirty-six books issued, but to identify every person of any consequence who worked on the project—writers, artists, editors—and to document every step of the process, from conception through gestation to delivery, culminating, finally, in a national conference mounted at the Library of Congress in 1996 to honor her accomplishment, and the ultimate gesture of approbation—publication by Oak Knoll Press in 2001 of a two-volume descriptive bibliography she wrote, titled, appropriately enough, *The Rivers of America*.

By concentrating on what are known as association copies, Jay Fliegelman, a professor of English at Stanford University, took a decidedly unorthodox approach to researching a thorough history of every book in his collection, detailing the way each impacted the life of the individuals who owned and handled them. "I am looking for the presence of the past in the present," is the way he described his efforts to me, and front and center in his queries was tireless research on the individual artifacts themselves, most poignantly, in my view, the story-behind-the-story of his copy of *My Bondage and My*

Freedom (1855). Inscribed by the author, Frederick Douglass, to Ellen Richardson, the British woman, Douglass wrote inside, "through whose active benevolence" he was "ransomed from American slavery." From Fliegelman's research into the background of his own books, which were supported by a grant from the American Antiquarian Society in Worcester, Massachusetts, will emerge a work he has tentatively titled *Belongings: Dramas of American Book Ownership, 1660–1860*.

In keeping with the subject of a work he is writing on multitalented people such as Pliny the Elder, Leonardo da Vinci, and Thomas Jefferson, Minor Myers Jr., an amateur musician and president of Illinois Wesleyan University, has collections that reflect a plentitude of interests, most notably the eighteenth century and anything it contains. One area in particular involves sheet music of long forgotten and sometimes long lost compositions that he can arrange and play with a musical ensemble composed of students at his college.

And finally there is Rolland Comstock, one of the most unorthodox collectors I have ever met, a person who is not content with possessing the books he loves, but takes his passion to the next level by crisscrossing the continent for face-to-face meetings with the authors he so greatly admires, and then defies every conventional rule of acquisition by buying multiple copies of a favored book, sometimes by the hundreds, if they are in jeopardy of being consigned to the remainder tables. Folly? Many would say so, but as far as Comstock is concerned, "If one rare book is good, then ten rare books must be ten times as good." And what makes his judgment seem prescient is the fact that so many of his authors have matured into talents of the first rank, some of them, like the English novelist Jim Crace, winning top literary awards on both sides of the Atlantic, with the result that those discards of a couple years ago are now being sought by collectors of modern first editions.

My interest in the scholarly element of book hunting extends further to the dealers I have met in my travels. How it is that a person becomes a knowledgeable professional in antiquarian books is just as vague an alchemy to comprehend as it is for the influences that create a collector, and oftentimes just as perplexing. The examples of two people who have made the transition in striking fashion, people I have not written about before because it also happens they are close friends of mine, seem especially apt in a book I have chosen to title *Among the Gently Mad*. Perhaps, in fact, it is for that very reason alone, because both of these friends—Robert C. Bradbury and Steven J. Schuyler—are contemporaries who have been only too eager to share with me what they know about books on a regular basis, not in a mentor-apprentice relationship, rather one of sharing among kindred spirits, with each side gleaning something meaningful from the other.

Bob Bradbury and I have known each other for twenty years, our friendship going back to the days when we were beginning our first terms on the board of the Friends of Goddard Library at Clark University. Working closely with Cushing C. Bozenhard—another collector who served on the board, and now, in retirement, the owner of Ex Libris Books of Shrewsbury, Massachusetts—and Jim Visbeck, the owner of Isaiah Thomas Books in Cotuit on Cape Cod, yet another of our colleagues, we organized our own antiquarian fair to benefit the library. For five heady years we set up shop each spring for one day in the university gymnasium, with every fair falling on what turned out to be a gorgeous Saturday afternoon in early May, exactly the kind of day that New Englanders unhesitatingly choose to spend outdoors after a long dreary winter, not inside the steamy confines of a basketball court. The turnout, as a consequence, was never anything to shout about, but we always had a respectable number of dealers who agreed to participate, none of them superstars, but solid booksellers from around the region all the same, with an interesting mix of goods to offer. They didn't come so much to sell as they did to buy for their own inventory, and not just from each other, but from us, since we had our own booth stocked with contributions from people who opened up their attics for the cause, donating a treasure trove of totally unpredictable and fresh material that always occasioned a feeding frenzy of interest at the opening bell. Working together on the Clark University fairs, it wasn't long before Bob and I were going out on booking trips together, not unlike the excursions I had enjoyed with my friend Raymond.

As a professor in the Graduate School of Management at Clark, Bradbury had a day job, but his recreational interests were focused on what he called his Literature of Birding Adventures collection, "not a collection *about* birds," he was always quick to point out, but one that concentrated on the accounts of such ornithological stalwarts as Roger Tory Peterson and James Fisher's *Wild America,* a 1955 record of their thirty-thousand-mile journey around the continent in search of the rarest of the rare. Few of the books in this collection had cost Bradbury very much money and were remarkable mostly for their comprehensiveness, which derived mainly from the work he had done to define the genre. "I had about a thousand books, and I was actively working on a bibliography," he recalled. "I had identified about fourteen hundred books altogether, so as a collector, there was still a ways for me to go. But then one day a dealer came in and offered me thirty-five thousand dollars for the collection, which was a heck of a lot more money than I had in it, so I took it on the spot. I took it mainly because I was ready for a change, and what I did was use the money to buy a fabulous collection of miniature books that was available right here in Worcester. It was the Achille St. Onge collection, and overnight I became a collector of some stature in the field of miniature books. I am a prime example of the guy who abandons one field of collecting and picks up another, and given my former specialty, I hesitate to say 'cold turkey,' but that's pretty much what happened. My wife, who is not a book collector, was thrilled with all the space I freed up at home. The guy who bought the bird books carted thirty boxes out of our house; I took the money he gave me and bought a collection that filled two shoe boxes."

Once Bradbury took up the pursuit of miniature books, he found very little in the way of published material to help him understand what he was looking for, so he proceeded to research and write two bibliographies of his own, becoming, in no small way, the leading American authority in the field. Just as interesting is that he approached the subject from a perspective that some might consider backwards, beginning in the here and now and moving chronologically toward the beginning, not the other way around. "I started in reverse because I thought it would be more interesting to locate principals who were alive, interview them, learn everything I could from them, and then take up the earlier examples that relied overwhelmingly on library research for documentation."

Bradbury's first book, *Twentieth Century United States Miniature Books* (North Clarendon, Vermont) was published in 2000, followed a year later by *Antique United States Miniature Books 1690–1900* (North Clarendon, Vermont). With a personal collection that has grown measurably over the past decade, Bradbury is still playing with "house money," as it were, supporting his activity by buying and selling among other collectors. "I don't have a cent of my own in miniature books beyond my initial investment," he said. "That thirty-five thousand dollars has been rolled over and over to the point that I now have six thousand volumes in my personal collection."

For the uninitiated—and they are legion in this genre—miniature books are real books in every sense of the word, with actual texts printed on high-quality paper and bound between hard covers, many of them elegant productions, but they are tiny volumes that are no more than three inches in height or width, and a mystery of existence to those who have never seen them before. "One question I can't answer is, 'Why miniature books?'" Bradbury said. But they have been with us for hundreds of years, and they have a devoted following. In his first book, Bradbury identified thirty-three hundred miniature books produced in the United States by 335 publishers during the twentieth century, two-thirds of them drawn from his own collection.

For the second bibliography, he used as his primary resources the holdings of the American Antiquarian Society in Worcester, and the Lilly Library of Indiana University in Bloomington, Indiana, detailing from their collections 1,625 miniature books produced by three hundred publishers issued over three centuries. In addition to handling the books, Bradbury scoured every published record and dealer's catalog he could find, tracked down every living printer, bookbinder, and publisher, and compiled biographical information. Easily his most significant finding was confirmation—and exact shelf location—of the oldest miniature book known to have been printed in North America, pushing back by fifteen years the date commonly accepted by book historians.

"I was reading everything I could find on the subject, and I came up with a journal reference from the 1920s that mentioned a particular title, and gave the location as the Boston Public Library," Bradbury said. "I went to the library, asked for the book, was told there was no such book, but I said, 'Look, please indulge me here, I even have call numbers for this.' So the woman went to the circulating stacks, and right there where it was supposed to be was this book wrapped in a cellophane envelope." A tiny volume of marriage advice called *A Wedding Ring,* the book was printed in Boston in 1690 by Samuel Green and published by Benjamin Harris, known today as the first newspaper publisher in America. As the only known copy of the book, the volume, needless to say, has been removed from general circulation and is now in the special collections unit of the Boston Public Library.

After tossing the idea of a career change around for a number of years, Bradbury decided early in 2002 to take early retirement from teaching and become a full-time bookseller specializing in miniature books, the transition being made especially easy by the success he had been experiencing buying, selling, trading, and building up a client list of three hundred customers on a recreational basis. Bradbury's reluctance to using the Web does not stem from indifference to the medium, but to the character of his customers. "People on the Internet tend *not* to be so concerned about condition, for one thing, and miniature-book customers are used to having their books come in a box in the mail, being able to feel them, read them, pick out what they want, and send back what they don't want. That would drive most dealers nuts, the idea of routinely sending four or five books out on approval, so people could look at them, handle them, experience them. I love it when my customers send books back to me, because that means they are choosing what they really like and adding them to their libraries, and that means in the future I am going to be able to sell more books to them. You develop a better bond with them this way."

I met Steve Schuyler in 1997 at the behest of Roger E. Stoddard, the distinguished curator of rare books at Houghton Library of Harvard University, and a mentor for both of us. Stoddard served as a kind of Socrates for me in the making of my books, suggesting areas that might make for fruitful inquiry, then reading what I wrote in manuscript. Schuyler got to know Stoddard in 1975 while doing research for his thesis, and while serving as the only graduate student on the Harvard Library Committee. Always a master at networking, Roger thought it a good idea that the two of us get together, and he arranged a lunch one afternoon in Cambridge.

"No good ever comes of gentle amateurs buying and selling," John Hill Burton warned in the nineteenth century in *The Book-Hunter.* "They will either be systematic losers, or they will acquire shabby, questionable habits, from which the professional dealers—on whom, perhaps, they look down—are exempt." Like Bradbury, Schuyler's path to leaving the ranks of the "gentle amateurs" and becoming a full-time bookseller—and thus avoiding the fate of being a "systematic loser"—was fortified by sustained periods of research but had its own digressions along the way. Like Bradbury, he too prepared for another career, earning a doctorate from Harvard University in Germanic languages and literatures with the idea of teaching. The subject of his dissertation—a study of the Jewish expatriate Kurt Wolff and his formation in 1942 of Pantheon Books as a publishing house in exile—brought him in contact with thousands of unpublished documents and, even more crucial, with dozens of people who shared their life experiences with him, particularly émigrés from Germany. "I helped a number of these people find homes for their books, and in the process of doing this I became an expert in the area of exile literature, the whole idea of what materials the émigrés took with them from Germany when they escaped the Nazis."

A series of interviews Schuyler conducted with the German expressionist Conrad Felixmüller (1897–1977) in 1974 as a Fulbright scholar in Berlin honed a passion for the fine arts, and occasioned a parallel specialty in that area, one that he pursues today in his business as a bookseller working out of his home in North Reading, Massachusetts. "I collect completely in the area of anything and everything to do with Conrad Felixmüller," Schuyler said. "He was like a grandfather to me, he gave me dozens of his graphics, and they formed the cornerstone of what has become an extensive collection, and the process is such, I believe, that he lives on as a creative force in a way through this enthusiastic collector, who happens to be me. Let me stress my belief here that he was aware of what has happening. I was in my twenties and was planning my return to Harvard and would channel my enthusiasm for his work into the next generation. It is a perfect example, I think, of the symbiosis that can exist between the artist and the collector. This was an important experience in my life, and collecting helps keep that alive." This belief was validated in 1997, on the occasion of Felixmüller's hundredth birthday, when Schulyer's interviews with him were published by the artist's family in a limited edition.

Another experience that hastened Schuyler along the path from hobbyist to book scout to bookseller was the year he spent in Cologne in 1963 as a high school exchange student living with a host family for whom books were a central part of daily life. "Werner Neite, my German father, was a psychologist who became the official historian of the city of Cologne. He also is a book person who took me everywhere, to flea markets, book fairs, book shops in London, and together we would find books. We saw so many cities through the windows of book shops, and today, when I do the Leipzig book fair, I fly into Cologne, get a rental car and take him with me and we work the show together; he is the gray-haired assistant at my booth."

Schuyler's decision to become a full-time bookseller was hastened along by the quantity of German-language materials he had begun to gather, and from the research he had done to document their importance. "Very few people in the United States have a clue as to what this material is. For me the Internet is an essential tool because how many people are going to come to my shed in North Reading to find German books? But there are people out there who are looking for the obscure materials I have sitting right here. The Internet has made the world my marketplace." As he became more and more involved in the material he was studying, Schuyler began writing about trends in the antiquarian world for a German publication, and in the United States for *AB Bookman's Weekly,* until its demise in 1999 the leading trade publication in the antiquarian world. In Schuyler's case, the opportunity to market what to most sensibilities would be arcane material became possible with the arrival of the Internet. As a full-time bookseller, he is now placing material with a number of institutions, most notably the United States Holocaust Memorial Museum in Washington, D.C., which has a mandate from Congress to build a major research collection. "What has pleased me enormously has been my ability to determine not only what books they do not have in their collections, but more importantly, to ascertain—and to convince the officials there—why there are certain books they absolutely have to have represented in their collections. It turns out that this library is the perfect repository for exactly the kinds of books brought to this country in the 1930s by the same German émigrés I interviewed twenty-five years ago for my dissertation."

Schuyler's most salient point—the point of this chapter, in fact—is the centrality of research in what he does. "Even a specialist can't possibly know everything about a subject, and making mistakes is very much a part of the learning process. When you're a book dealer there are millions and millions of books published during your lifetime; you can't possibly know them all, and I'm talking issue points now, bibliographical details, not just the importance of different works in your specialty. That's why I have tremendous respect for my European colleagues—because they have this tradition of scholarship in everything they do, they have a strong sense about their underpinnings. What they don't know, they research. There is a poem in German by Rainer Maria Rilke, with a line that roughly translates, 'Be ahead of all departure.' I interpret that to mean that you have to have a certain sense of timing in life; with regard to collecting, it behooves you to have a sense of what is happening, and to be prepared to move forward on your intuition."

Not every collector is going to have the formal training of doctoral research to drill them in the skills and conventions of formal scholarship, and to suggest that it is necessary is not my intention in citing these two examples. Instead, what I hope to impart is the idea of an attitude, an approach, that seems to be in order. If you are going to take on a project that involves the nuances of intellectual expression, then it makes sense that you do your homework. How a person goes about conducting research is a matter of individual preference, but anyone who knows how to use a catalog, anyone who knows how to browse through a stack of books, has the rudiments of a solid beginning. I happen to be a person who benefits greatly from footnotes in nonfiction works; I read the citations that authors give for their findings, and if the material is even remotely interesting to me, I follow up by going to the original sources.

What I have found to be enormously helpful in these wanderings are the major search engines on the Internet, with particular admiration for www.google.com. I heard Tim Berners-Lee, the Massachusetts Institute of Technology professor credited with creating the concept of the World Wide Web, tell a gathering of New England librarians in Boston in 1999 that, in his view, Google was the most sophisticated search engine he could recommend; that was about as authoritative a testimonial as I could imagine, and it has been my computer source of first resort ever since. Unlike the other search engines and Internet providers that pester you to death with pop-up advertisements and random clutter, Google is all about searching. The option to let the software pick out the one most important site or "address" of a particular file or image known as the URL (Universal Resource Locator) it "thinks" you're looking for—the "I'm feeling lucky" click—I find to be uncannily accurate, on target about 90 percent of the time, and remarkably helpful in teaching the creative application of key words in the search field. For providing an entry point into an area, Google is by itself an invaluable reference tool, one that is immediately accessible, and impressively successful in providing meaningful leads.

I can recall countless instances when I have typed in a few hopeful words and been rewarded with snapshot summaries of things I need to clarify or verify immediately, and with a minimum of disquietude. I have been appearing on the syndicated radio program *The Book Guys* every week since 1998 with Allan Stypeck, the owner of Second Story Books in Washington, D.C., and Bethesda, Maryland, and Mike Cuthbert, a professional radio personality of many years standing, and I always get the greatest kick out of being able to answer a caller's query within minutes, and more often than not I do it by punching a few key words into Google. Easily the most amusing were the results I got on a search prompted by a woman asking about a children's book published in the 1950s she vaguely remembered from her childhood as "churkendoose," and was eager to rediscover for her own children. I immediately typed that word in—thankfully, she had the spelling right—and got sixty-eight "hits"

for *The Churkendoose* by Ben Ross Berenberg with illustrations by Delwyn Cunningham, a charming tale about a bird
that is a cross between a chicken, a turkey, a duck, and a
goose, and quite popular, it turns out, among teachers interested in promoting tolerance, respect, and understanding for
those who are "different." Not only did I find the bibliographical information in a snap, I immediately determined
the availability of copies for sale on www.abebooks.com and
the range of prices being asked. This sort of discovery, these
kinds of results, would be impossible without these fabulous
databases. But as any experienced investigative journalist
will tell you, leads are leads, nothing more than a meaningful
first step that can tantalize and illuminate, sometimes even
deliver a sizeable chunk of the information that you need,
but for the determined book hunter, still not much more than
a "good start" all the same.

I have discussed in various chapters the idea of single
author collectors, a breed of book hunter, according to one
bibliophile of notable accomplishment who chooses to keep
his activity private, with "one-track minds." I laughed appre-
ciatively when this person used that phrase, since he is one of
the most acclaimed collectors of a particular author's works to
be found anywhere in the world, so he spoke with affection,
not derision. I mention the amusing exchange here because
this collector reminded me how endemic "single-culture societies" are to the world of the book hunter, and he urged me to
seek out a website he understood had been established as a
kind of clearinghouse for those interested in meeting up with,
in his words, their "bibliophilic soul mates." I found a number
of them, actually, once again, through Google, by using the
key words of "author," "fan," and "clubs." There were dozens

of hits; the best among them included: www.cygnus.uwa.edu. au/~amgraham/girlsown/clublist.html and www.bookbrowse. com/.

My guess is that a similar search for anyone—be it Mark Twain, Rudyard Kipling, Emily Brontë, Edgar Rice Burroughs, Isaac Asimov, Edith Wharton, the canonical mainstays as well as the precious few—would be fairly certain to find them represented, and not only in "chat rooms" populated by gatherings of acolytes, but in seriously organized single-author societies that post important biographical and bibliographical material—specific listings, in other words, of the kinds of things that a serious book hunter ought to be looking for. Whatever the object of your affection, you can be pretty sure that you are not alone, and chances are that somebody has already posted exactly the kind of information you need on the Web—and there is the additional prospect of hooking up with people who share your particular passion.

I offer as evidence the fruits of one such search, taking no more than fifteen minutes to find all of the relevant links I needed to get fully on track. It happens that I am a tremendous admirer of the writings of Winston Churchill, the only professional politician to win a Nobel Prize for literature (and deservedly so), and carried out a sequence of Google searches with "Churchill" as my primary key word with a constantly changing variety of others—"collect," "books," "bibliophile," "bibliomania," "first editions" were some of them—to refine the yield down to manageable selections. I found my way to www.winstonchurchill.org/ and an essay by a man named Wallace Johnson, titled, "Bibliomania Revisited." He begins: "Several years have passed since I first began my correspondence with Churchill bibliophiles to learn about their collections, personalities and peculiarities." In the next paragraph he notes how he quickly discovered what he always suspected: "We do not stand alone. Many others from diverse regions in the English-speaking world share our enthusiasm." Wallace, I promptly learned, is the author of another essay, "Bibliomania and the Literary Churchill," which appeared in *Finest Hour,* the official journal of the Churchill Center and International Churchill Societies, which has its home page at this very site I had located through my searches. Probing further, I found mention of a number of prominent Churchillians, one of whom, a bookseller named Richard M. Langworth, had established his own site, www.churchillbooks.com, which is dedicated exclusively to books by and about "the Man of the Century," and includes multiple other pertinent references. What I am demonstrating here is how one thing leads to another, and that by following the leads and the links that were right in front of me, I then came up with a superb essay written by Langworth, titled, appropriately enough, "What Price Churchill? Building a Collection," which I recommend heartily to anyone who needs to be persuaded that collecting is possible at *any* level. Langworth begins by repeating a question he is asked all the time: What does it cost to own a complete set of Churchill's books? He writes:

> The answer is: between $1500/£1000 and well over $100,000/£67,000, depending on the varieties, editions and conditions desired. Then, if you can find them, add another $100,000 for first editions of the two rare, probable vanity press productions, *Mr. Brodrick's Army* and *For Free Trade.* (You might have to

add even more; the last Brodrick sale I know of was in 1999 for $75,000/£50,000.) And this is for books not inscribed by our author.

Langworth then gives learned advice on how to go about building respectable Churchill collections at every level of sophistication. His focus, of course, is entirely on his hero, but the principle at work applies to every single-author aficionado. The suggestion to "avoid books rebound in leather" is backed up with this explanation:

> A collector once asked me to take his complete Churchill collection on consignment. At great expense over the years, he had rebound each first edition, many of which were fine originals, in full morocco leather. The bindings were beautiful. He was astonished when I said that for a specialist dealing mainly with advanced collectors, these books were virtually unsaleable. All I could recommend was that he consign them to an auction house or a big city dealer specializing in fine bindings (and pray a lot).

The central point of Langworth's essay—how to collect successfully on a budget—is stated forthwith: "Set Your Goal and Stick with It." I don't know how to express it more succinctly myself.

CHAPTER 8

BOOKING THE WORLD

By far the most significant book-hunting development to come along in recent years has been computer technology, not only for the way it has challenged the artifactual relevance of the traditional codex itself, but for the profound degree to which it has refined the process of discovery and acquisition. For those unimaginative few who find little pleasure in turning up material in the field, it is possible now to collect entirely over the Internet, and there are several websites that support this approach most capably. Through the process of attrition, the site of choice for those so disposed has become the Advanced Book Exchange, where, at last count, the inventories of nine thousand dealers comprising some 40 million books were said to be in the database, and I have seen little in my frequent searches of www.abebooks.com to dispute that contention. It is a fantastic site, and extremely fast, which is why it is my favorite, although I have great affection as well for www.addall.com, in essence a search engine that is programmed to comb other search engines (including www.abebooks.com) for your queries, and to give you a balanced readout of choices from the myriad that are available, and the somewhat slower, but all the same admirable capabilities of www.bookfinder.com, which performs many of the same functions. The potential of such resources is obvious, especially for comparison shoppers intent on establishing a price range for various titles, and for those who want to contact dealers directly, not through an intermediary, which is the case with www.alibris.com (the successor to www. interloc.com), which adds what amounts to a handling fee to the cost of books it brokers from other dealers. There also is www.bibliofind.com, once the premier site for used, out-of-print, and rare books, but since being absorbed into the larger matrix of www.amazon.com a few years ago, now little more than a bit player on the margins, especially since independent dealers are no longer allowed to list their books with them.

Regardless of the search engine that is used—and browsers should take a good look at the innovative sites of some individual booksellers as well—scores of them can be found at www.abaa.org, the home page of the Antiquarian Booksellers Association of America (ABAA), and www.ilab-lila.com, home page of the International League of Antiquarian Booksellers/Ligue Internationale de la Librairie Ancienne (ILAB/ LILA)—a decidedly new day has dawned not only for the book-buying public, but for the way traditional booksellers now go about their business. What is truly exciting is that instead of being limited to "booking the heartland" of one particular region on any particular day, as Jack Matthews called the exercise in an enjoyable book devoted to the time-honored exercise of scouting books the old-fashioned way, today's bibliophile has the capacity to "book" the planet in a matter of minutes without ever having to leave home. The downside to this is that since, generally speaking, you go into one of these databases in search of a specific title, it involves very little in the way of adventure or discovery, and zero opportunity to examine the merchandise before placing an order, an always advisable routine to follow when pondering previously owned and handled material that is being described in terms that reflect a subjective point of view. Of even greater concern is the impact the development is having on what is known in the trade as the "open shop," with more and more dealers finding they can make a decent living by doing all of their transactions over the Internet, and thereby eliminating entirely the ritual of allowing customers the privilege of rummaging through their stock. It even allows people who might not otherwise have the resources to be booksellers in the first place to offer material for sale from their homes or backyard sheds; all that is needed is a small inventory of books to sell, and a website to market them. Indeed, the cost of listing up to five hundred books with www.abebooks.com in the spring of 2002 was twenty-five dollars a month, a negligible expense for an aspiring dealer; seasoned professionals have options that allow many more postings, topping out at three hundred dollars a month for 150,000 listings and above.

"What I think the Internet did more than anything else is make the dividing line between bookseller and collector more vague than it has ever been," Steven J. Schuyler told me, and as a bookseller who gravitated into the business full-time after having dabbled agreeably for some years as a semiprofessional, he was including himself in the evaluation. "What you have now are a lot of collectors who fancy themselves as being book scouts. You find this especially to be the case with people who have built strong collections by constantly upgrading their copies, and are looking for profitable ways to get rid of their inferior copies. In the old days these people might sell their duplicates to dealers, or use them in trade with other collectors. Now, they look around, they say to themselves, 'Hey, I can do this,' and bingo, they're in business. It costs them next to nothing to get up on the web, and then you've got eBay on top of that, where anyone can be a seller, and suddenly you have an operation going. Personally, I would say that this sort of thing is useful to people who haven't got a clue about what's going on, and it really works for the pretty mundane, ordinary stuff." Another bookseller— a prominent ABAA member, in fact, who for obvious reasons chose to make the following observation without direct attribution—put the matter in finer perspective: "I concentrate on putting stuff on my website that I am unable to sell otherwise, and by no means my high-end things. It's a great way to unload your mistakes." What this bookseller means by "mistakes," of course, is not material that is "wrong" in any bibliographical way, but material that perhaps was bought for too high a price and needs to be sold to someone—anyone— who might be interested, or material that has been gathering dust for years, waiting to be discovered by the "right" suitor.

Still, for all these perceived shortcomings, a person would have to be a total Luddite to dismiss the worth of these extraordinary devices, and the truth of the matter is that I use them often, dozens of times a week, in fact, but only rarely to buy what might be regarded in any conventional sense as *rar-*

ities or *collectibles,* unless, of course, it is to acquire a title that I had never expected to see anywhere, let alone one that I have discovered through this technology is available for immediate purchase. One of the most frequently asked questions in recent years—indeed, it has become the most exhausting to deal with—is whether or not the overwhelming influence of computer technology has dealt a mortal blow to the viability of the printed book and altered forever the ways people go about acquiring them. My answer to that is this: The Internet is a wondrous thing, and anyone who fails to take advantage of its applications is missing out on a powerful new tool. The functionality of this extraordinary resource is obvious, and it has had an undeniable impact on the way institutional libraries today are building their academic and research collections. For the private book hunter, the computer is a new way to scout out the field, to make contact with booksellers, to conduct research, to establish value. It is unequaled in its ability to fill out a desideratum, or want list—getting books that you already know you want to have and thought you would never find—and unsurpassed in furnishing an immediate link to locating corroborative information. Using the resources of this technology properly, today's collector can run a tighter, more finely focused operation, sometimes explore frontiers that might otherwise forever remain terra incognita. I have turned up books that in years past would have taken me months to find, and in many cases may well have eluded me entirely. I have found the medium to be an extraordinary way to locate copies of books that I need for my research, books, in some cases, that are not readily available in nearby research libraries, or if available there, cannot be removed from the premises.

The larger truth of the matter, too, is that I like to own my own copies of the books I use as primary references, and one of my favorite personal collections is comprised of the books I have used as source materials in my writing. I regard it as no small accomplishment to say that fully 95 percent of the books I list in the bibliography of *A Gentle Madness* come from my home library—and that bibliography, I should point out, is thirty-seven pages long—and I can make the same claim for about half of what I cite in *Patience & Fortitude,* with a concerted effort afoot to locate the titles that remain. I would not even consider such an undertaking if I did not have www.abebooks.com, www.addall.com, or www. bookfinder.com to help me get there. It is true that most of my books about books—my copy of Thomas Frognall Dibdin's *Bibliographical Decameron* (1817) in three volumes, the selective catalog of Harry Widener's library, privately printed two years before his death on the *Titanic* in 1912, my full run of the essential British quarterly, the *Book Collector,* some two hundred numbers going back fifty years, come immediately to mind—were acquired from professional booksellers, in the instance of these materials, Colophon Books in New Hampshire and Oak Knoll Books in New Castle, Delaware, both specialists in bibliography and the book arts. Many others were total surprises to me the moment I found them in secondhand bookstores, most notably my copies of Robert Curzon's *Visits to Monasteries of the Levant* (1849) and Mrs. James T. Fields's *A Shelf of Old Books* (1894), both of which have proven most useful to me in my writing. And then there are the multitude of penetrating works I come across in the stacks of research libraries, essential titles such as John Willis Clark's *The Care of Books* (1901) and James Westfall Thompson's *The Medieval Library* (1939), books that impress me so much that I will not rest until I have my own copies, and it is here that the computer has proved its true mettle. In cases like this, I know exactly what I am looking for, and I learn quickly how many copies are "out there" being listed for sale, and it is extraordinary just how many obscure books there *are* abundantly available now in the world. On those occasions that multiple copies of the same title are for sale, I can compare prices and condition, and make a fast transaction. One of my most pleasant surprises came when I determined during an interview with the librarian of Hampshire College in western Massachusetts that I had to have a copy of *The Making of a Library: The Academic Library in Transition* (1972) by Robert S. Taylor. I have no idea how many copies of this forgotten monograph were issued when it was published three decades ago, but it could not have been very many, since even Hampshire College, at the time of publication a fledgling college, and the subject of the author's study, had to scurry about the country to find a backup copy for its own permanent collections. What made the book interesting to me was Taylor's bold predictions of a "future library" devoid of books, quite a proposition to consider in the days before the Internet, and as history has shown, for all the wrong reasons. I found what may well have been the only copy for sale in America in 1999 through www.abebooks.com, and I happily paid a dealer in Houston, Texas, twenty dollars to acquire it.

But a curious anomaly has emerged in the way this tool is achieving success, one that reaffirms the preference most bibliophiles have for handling the goods in advance of closing a deal, especially when the goods in question involve the expenditure of serious money. Just about every bookseller maintains a website today, and most of them offer a good deal of their inventory on-line, but the best dealers still issue printed catalogs, and not for reasons of sentimentality—these are fairly expensive to produce and distribute, after all—but because they continue to perform a worthwhile function.

"I would say that fifty percent of my business is now done on-line," William S. Reese of New Haven, Connecticut, told me, and that is quite a statement to make, considering that he is the world's leading dealer in Americana. But that 50 percent of his business, Reese was quick to point out, accounts for only 10 or 15 percent of gross sales, meaning that the big-ticketed items, which he is internationally celebrated for providing to his most important customers—treasures that have included several copies of the 1493 Columbus Letter, an Eliot Bible, numerous Federalist Papers, the list of high spots he has acquired and sold goes on and on—are still handled directly with his clients. "I have a sense that every book over a hundred dollars has to be listed in a printed catalog," Reese said. "This doesn't mean we won't put valuable material up on the web, we certainly will, and we do, with varying degrees of success, but there is a certain validity, I think, that is associated with the traditional catalog. People are paying you good money for your judgment and your analysis, and they want to see that reflected in your written descriptions, and there should be a degree of permanence to those descriptions, which is something you achieve with a printed catalog."

Perhaps nowhere is that sentiment emphasized more dramatically than in the catalogs of the Swiss-based bookseller Heribert Tenschert, the world's leading dealer in illuminated manuscripts of the Middle Ages and the Renaissance, material that by definition is unique, and is priced, as a consequence, in the thousands, sometimes millions, of dollars. Tenschert told me that the world market for the great majority of this material consists of no more than thirty people, affluent people who come to his elegant shop on a crystalline tributary of the Rhine River near the German border to be convinced in person that these exquisite objects are worthy of their affection. Yet he still believes he must prepare elaborate catalogs for their examination, expensive productions that he sells as beautiful books to others he realizes will never own the treasures themselves. "People who know me know they can trust everything I write about these books," he said, "and they know they can buy them on the strength of the descriptions. But most of them still like coming here and having the books laid out in front of them." Tenschert has an attractive website, with links in English, German, and French, but the purpose clearly is to inform, not to market, to entice, but other than the catalogs themselves, not to sell.

Allen Ahearn and his wife, Patricia, the owners of Quill & Brush bookstore in Dickerson, Maryland, specialize in first editions of twentieth-century literature, and have compiled three editions of the authoritative reference, *Collected Books: The Guide to Values*. They also have been issuing price guides since 1975, and have tracked the impact the Internet has had on book buying, noting along the way trends and tendencies that have taken place. "For a couple of years there, 1997, '98, '99, all the dealers became intoxicated with the Internet, and a lot of us stopped doing catalogs for awhile," he said. "We didn't have time really, we were putting everything we had up on the web and everybody else was doing the same thing, and the fact is that everybody was busy selling all the stuff that they'd had lying around for twenty years. I mean, you could actually see this in the trade. There were some catalogs out there, but it really dropped off dramatically. Now? Well, by 1999, I think we all began to realize that the Internet was just another part of the business, and most of us who were doing the catalogs before are now doing them again. Why? Because there is no serendipity on the Internet, number one, and there are good customers who don't look on the Internet."

In midtown Manhattan, the Argosy Book Store occupies all six floors of a building on Madison Avenue for the express purpose of selling used books, rare books, and prints, a luxury in this prime location that is made possible by the fact that the family that owns the business also owns the real estate. "For us, it's not selling books if you don't have contact with the customers," Judith Lowry told me, explaining why she and her two sisters have turned down numerous offers to sell the building purchased by her late father, Louis Cohen, in 1964 for one hundred thousand dollars—a sum that, today, would be about half of what they might have to pay each month in rent to occupy the same property, a reality of contemporary urban life that underscores why the open shop is an endangered species in so many large cities. In addition to being their own landlord—a circumstance that also allows Fred Bass and his daughter Nancy Bass to operate the Strand Book Store on Broadway and Twelfth in Greenwich Village, and for decades allowed the owners of the famed Gotham Book Mart at 41 West Forty-seventh Street, founder Frances Steloff and her successor, Andreas Brown, to do the same—Lowry said that another reason why she and her sisters are able to continue serving the public directly is because of the business they generate on their website. This accounts for half of their gross sales and has enabled them to place obscure material they thought would never sell with new customers, people, in many cases, who have never even been to New York. "Books that have been on the shelf for thirty years, suddenly we are getting orders for them from all over the world," she said. Because of the Internet, the kind of books the Argosy is buying now has changed as well. "We are buying fewer ordinary books these days, just good books," and in Lowry's lexicon, a *good* book is a book that she would price at one hundred dollars or more.

Beyond the gadgetry and the instant access that have influenced *how* people collect are the ways in which the computer has changed *what* people collect—a concept that, truth be known, I find far more interesting to consider. While the essence of book collecting in the twenty-first century is still driven by the same basic principles as before, there has been a refinement in the *kinds* of things that people are interested in gathering. With so much information now available on-line and in other forms—compact discs, microfilm, and the like— many collectors have become far more selective, contenting themselves with the certified high spots and disdaining the lesser works of certain authors. The same dynamic is evident in areas where it is subjects, not specific authors, that are being collected, because there too information is readily available elsewhere. A similar shift is apparent among institutional libraries. As recently as fifty years ago, there was little distinction made between books and information; the gathering of books was undertaken for the purpose of gathering knowledge, and on the university level, the culture of books and the culture of education were synonymous.

Indeed, the great research libraries in America today

maintain what are known as special collections—vast holdings of rare books, in other words—which were gathered and preserved as often as not through the efforts of private collectors, a phenomenon that was a central theme of my 1995 book, *A Gentle Madness,* and which was the subject of a forum mounted at the Library of Congress in April 2001 to discuss strategies for new partnerships in light of these developments. One of the participants in the forum, Bill Reese, went so far as to assert that "most antiquarian books in the world are now in institutions," and that the greatest problem he faces as a dealer is in finding exceptional material to buy for his clients. "The attics have largely been cleaned out," he said. "Rare books as generally defined are now uncommon; in good condition, they are *very* rare." In numerous interviews with me over the years, Reese has elaborated on that point, noting that the most time he spends on any single activity, by far, is on buying books. "Selling them is the easy part," he said. "Finding them is what is hard."

Reese is talking, of course, about material at the highest end of the spectrum in traditional areas of interest, and what he says should not discourage today's collectors—in fact it should encourage them to develop new avenues they can explore for themselves. The half dozen Shakespeare folios still in private hands may well remain in private hands for the foreseeable future, but the circle of ownership is so exclusive that most people who collect books will never have an opportunity to enter it in any case. That's a fact of life. But the enduring beauty of this exercise is that anyone can play. That was the reality a hundred years ago; it is the reality today. Reese began his Washington remarks, in fact, by lamenting that as much as he would dearly like to purchase a copy of the Bay Psalm Book—produced in Cambridge, Massachusetts, in 1639, it was the first book printed in British North America—he knows the likelihood of that ever happening is next to nil, even for those privileged few who could afford the seven-figure sum that would be necessary to secure it, since only eleven copies are known, and all are installed in institutional collections. Like the Shakespeare First Folio of 1623, the Bay Psalm Book is an iconic artifact, revered as much for what it represents as for what it contains. On lower rungs of the ladder, where the sums being spent are not in the millions of dollars, a similar phenomenon is also in evidence, as prices that just five years ago would have been considered unthinkable are increasingly in evidence—thirty-three thousand dollars for a copy of Harper Lee's 1964 novel, *To Kill a Mockingbird,* and the exact same amount for J. D. Salinger's *Catcher in the Rye,* at one New York auction in 2001, to cite just two examples.

Obviously, if it is the universally acclaimed prizes you are after, then you will be paying dearly for the privilege of ownership. But for the general population of bibliophiles, there are still fulfilling paths to explore, and for many, the Internet is helping shape the way they are now going about the task. Viewed as a powerful tool, the computer has the capacity to intensify the pleasure of collecting, in some cases creating opportunities that otherwise might be impossible to consider. I cite by way of example the experiences of a good friend and neighbor of mine, a fellow writer, with her husband, the author Nicholas Gage, longtime enthusiasts of the New England antiques shops, flea markets, and trade shows. For years, a consuming passion of Joan's has been daguerreotypes, the earliest form of photography perfected by the Frenchman

Louis Jacques Mandé Daguerre in 1839, a process that became tremendously popular in the United States, especially in the making of family portraits. Within months of its introduction, studios had opened throughout the country, and remained popular until the outbreak of the Civil War, by which time two notable advancements in technique—the ambrotype, which is a negative image on glass, and the tintype, which allowed for multiple copies to be produced from a single negative—marked the end of this pioneering era.

It is impossible to exaggerate the influence of daguerreotypes in the mid-nineteenth century. Millions of likenesses were produced, most of them of people posing in studios, others picturing outdoor scenes and cityscapes that have long since vanished. Produced from an image that was imprinted on a shimmering silvered surface coated onto a copper plate, the process was such that no exact copies could be made from the originals, and because each was therefore unique, the element of scarcity ultimately entered the equation, with rarity not too far behind. People who covet "dags," as they are familiarly called by their aficionados, are an impassioned species of collector, and have their own network of support groups, organizations, specialist dealers, and favored techniques of acquisition. A savvy "picker" with a fine eye for quality and nuance, Joan Gage has enhanced her fascination for these historical artifacts by seeking out materials that give vitality to people whose names are no longer known, people whose identities exist only as images etched on glass or metal plates a century and a half ago by sunlight and chemicals. "I am mindful of the fact that what I am holding is probably the only record of their existence," Gage said, indicating dozens upon dozens of images lying about the office in her home where most are catalogued, itemized by subject, and wherever possible, researched on the Internet for further documentation. "I am the only one alive who knows, the only one who cares, that these people existed. I believe that every dag has a story to tell, but because they are so far removed from us historically, we have lost the ability to interpret what is being told. That is what I am trying to redress by getting books."

Because the making of a daguerreotype was a time-consuming process, static scenes involving no movement were arranged in the portrait studios, often involving the use of clamps to keep the head rigid, and props, frequently books, as one way of making sure the hands did not move. Most daguerreotypes are small, and because the technology to invert the image was several years away from being developed, the pictures appear in reverse—the original negative, in other words. Writing, as a consequence, appears backwards, and the titles of books, where they appear, have to be deciphered. Using a magnifying instrument known as jeweler's loupe, what Gage has done is decipher the titles of the books she finds in so many of the portraits she has acquired, understanding all the while that many of them are little more than props used by the photographer, but feeling just the same that knowing something of the books being depicted can tell her more about the subjects.

"There's a lot of scholarship that remains to be done in the field of American daguerreotypes," she said. "You'll see that the European daguerreotypes tend to follow the fashions that were in vogue among European painters, very stylized. The Americans strike more frontal poses, like American folk art, primitive art. In dags, there are many areas where you have tremendous latitude to figure things out for yourself. To give you just one example, you frequently see boys dressed as girls because that was the fashion, but how do you tell a boy from a girl in one of these pictures? Most dag collectors know that the key clue comes in the part of the hair. With the boys, it's on the side, and with the girls it's down the middle. Or if the child is holding a horse whip, it's a boy; if it's a doll, it's a girl. After you start looking at these things by the hundreds, you begin to see patterns, and I believe that every object in the picture is telling you something. You will see quite a few pictures, for instance, where people are holding large, prominent handkerchiefs. What does that mean? Well, after looking at hundreds of them, I have developed a theory that this is a way of telling us that someone has died, and those are photographs of people in mourning."

The dags with books pictured present some other opportunities that Gage has pursued to enhance her collection, strategies made possible by the tremendous research capabilities of the computer. Examination of a portrait of a woman holding a book, upside down, and with the title reversed, disclosed the title, *Pictorial History of the American Revolution*. An on-line search located a copy of such a book, written by Robert Sears, published in 1845, and, when it arrived, bearing the same pictorial cloth cover, gold-stamped on brown fabric. Another search was a bit more difficult, because only a few words of the title—"Squadron" and "Voyage Around the World"—could be deciphered. There also was the name, "George Read." Gage's queries turned up *Around the World: A Narrative of a Voyage in the East India Squadron Under Commodore George C. Read by an Officer of the U. S. Navy*, in two volumes, New York, 1840, a copy of which she found on-line for twenty-eight dollars. A portrait of two girls, pre-sumably sisters, each holding a book, led to the purchase of an identical vocabulary primer. Another of a distinguished-looking man standing next to a volume titled *Patent Office Report 1831* raised more questions than it answered. Is he an inventor? What did he invent? Is it listed in that book? "These books are interesting to me because they are telling us some-thing about these people, who they were, what they found important," Gage said. The next step will involve the use of technology. "Some of these titles I just can't make out, and I am confident that I will get a program at some point that I can use to enlarge these images and clarify the title. Then I'll go out and find those books, too."

Gage does a good deal of her scouting these days on www.eBay.com, the on-line auction site she described to me as a place "where just about anything goes, and just about everything does." What she tells me about eBay is what every other collector I know who shops there says: the site offers fantastic opportunities to capitalize on the follies of others. The obvious downside to this is that people who have no conception of what it is they are selling are just as likely to post descriptions that overstate the condition or importance of an item as they are to miss entirely its true significance. Gage will not hesitate to contact sellers directly and pose questions about daguerreotypes she is bidding on, and what she frequently finds are people who are probing her for infor-mation on what *she* thinks it is they have. "When a seller asks me how to identify a photo—how to know if it's a daguer-reotype, an ambrotype, or a tintype, I always e-mail them a page of information I have prepared for this purpose. But if sellers do not ask for help and clearly have misidentified or underestimated what they're selling, experienced buyers can score an extremely good buy. The trick is telling people who really don't know from those who are simply playing dumb to fire a buyer's acquisitive greed. Usually the misidentification is an honest mistake, and on the few occasions that I thought I bought a dag and discovered when it came that it was only a tintype, the buyer has always offered to return my money or lower the price."

Another eBay regular, Gordon A. Pfeiffer of Wilmington, Delaware, has been collecting what he likes to call "historical confetti" for more than thirty years, but has found new opportunities that would never materialize if not for the on-line option. An amateur historian, Pfeiffer described this particular collecting interest—one of several he pursues, the others following more conventional tracks—as comprising ephemeral materials that give some texture to the rich history of his home state. He takes special pleasure in gathering nineteenth-century broadsides, handbills, tickets, circulars, trade cards, letterheads, posters, and the like.

"I have had great success on eBay, because I know what I'm looking for," the retired banker and president of the Delaware Bibliophiles told me at the twenty-fifth anniversary dinner of the organization early in 2002. "As a boy I started as a coin collector, but my mother was a librarian, and I have always had books in my life, and when I graduated from college my interests changed." For years, Pfeiffer did his rummaging at flea markets, book fairs, and ephemera shows, and he always had a standard line when asked about his specific interests. "I never know what I'm looking for until I see it, those are the first words out of my mouth," Pfeiffer said. That kind of attitude was a plus when he began looking for material on-line in 1999, and there is a specific routine he now follows on eBay. "I will type in *Delaware,* and then I will *minus* out certain words that I want to subtract from my search. I'm not interested in Delaware *quarters,* for instance, so I will minus out 'quarter,' 'quarters,' 'roll,' and then I subtract out other things that pop up frequently like *Delaware Gap* and *Hudson,* because I get Delaware and Hudson Railroad often, and I don't want them either. I limit a good number of common things like that. What I end up with is somewhere around six hundred hits, and then I look through them to see if a title catches my eye. What I find with eBay, quite frankly, is stuff that I've never seen before." Pfeiffer included among his favorite discoveries a Brandywine stereoscopic view of a DuPont powder mill and an invitation to a Wilmington party, held on the deck of a ship just a few days before the crash of 1929. And what's the most he has spent on any of these items? "Not a lot," he said, "never more than three hundred dollars for any single purchase," which is about the maximum Joan Gage said she has ever spent on a daguerreotype. "How far I am willing to go would depend a lot on what I know about the dealer, because you do get to know who they are after a while, and it would depend on just how much I wanted the item. I go on-line every six days to do a full search, but I'm looking at it every day."

For all this newfound liberation, Pfeiffer made clear that he remains a traditionalist in pursuit of books, with particular interest in the influence the British designer William Morris had on American printing, and in gathering examples of American trade bindings. In addition to the Delaware Bibliophiles, Pfeiffer also serves as president of the Delaware

Historical Society, and to sharpen his skills as a collector, he has taken two courses at Rare Book School in Charlottesville, Virginia. "My philosophy is that you look, you learn, you listen, you pay attention," Pfeiffer said. "That is a discipline that never changes."

CHAPTER 9

STRUTTING YOUR STUFF

As I move periodically among the gently mad, the most persistent complaint I hear is how difficult it is for bibliophiles to persuade nonbelievers that they have lives outside of their libraries, or that they actually *enjoy* themselves when they are alone with their prized possessions. Indeed, if there is any single experience I can count on when I am giving talks at university libraries or meeting with book-collecting groups, it is the certainty that I will be invited to someone's home to see objects that they are unwilling to share with those who have little interest in collecting, particularly if the artifacts they are so wild about happen to be printed on paper and bound between hard covers. "People who don't collect are civilians" is the way one good friend of mine, a Marine Corps veteran who collects diaries, correspondence, journals, and accounts of the Civil War, explains it, and there is wisdom in his hard-nosed comment. I cannot pinpoint exactly why this is, but my guess is that unlike every other collectible object, books are impressive for reasons that very rarely meet the naked eye. Some of this may well be due to the fact that whatever "sex appeal" a book may have comes from the "inner beauty" of its text, not the "outer shell" of its appearance. This is not to say that books are not beautiful to behold—a good many of them are breathtaking—but it is the content, above all else, and the reception the works have merited, that imparts resonance. A person who has no interest in American fiction is not likely to be excited at the prospect of seeing a first issue copy of William Faulkner's *Soldier's Pay* in original wraps, though there might be an incredulous flicker of curiosity if a recent auction figure of forty-five thousand dollars is mentioned. Even then, boredom is sure to set in before long, and the conversation will move to other areas, unless of course someone asks what *Harry Potter and the Philosopher's Stone* is going for these days, and is told that a first issue copy of the 1997 fantasy went at auction in 2001 for fifteen thousand dollars, which will let loose another flurry of bemused disbelief. Other than sporadic episodes such as these, however, book collectors have learned to choose their moments, and to choose them with care.

I will never forget the Sunday afternoon in 1989 that I spent in the rambling colonial home of Leonard and Lisa Baskin in western Massachusetts, a day devoted to the handling and appreciation of one magnificent rarity after another in a variety of compelling fields. A widely respected artist, sculptor, and fine-press bookmaker, Baskin, who died in 2000 at the age of seventy-five, was also a noted printmaker proficient in creating woodcuts, wood engravings, etchings, aquatints, and lithographs, and his collecting interests, which had begun in childhood, had a tendency to "cover the waterfront," as he put it. His wife, Lisa, not only shared many of his collecting passions, but pursued her own specialties independently of him, primarily in the area of women's history and literature. In addition to a wide variety of illustrated books and prints, they had gathered Renaissance medals, bronzes, casts, memorial jewelry, and every manner of graphic material. "Do you know what watch papers are?" Leonard asked me at one point, and proceeded to show me a huge gathering of tiny notes, each engraved with the name of a watchmaker, and each bearing a small watercolor, a common custom in the eighteenth and nineteenth centuries. "We don't collect bookplates because *everybody* collects bookplates, but we do collect booksellers' and bookbinders' tickets," he continued, and then there were circulating-library tickets and old ferry tickets nearby for us to poke through. As we examined these assorted materials, the hours flew by, and as I began to feel that I was imposing on their hospitality, the Baskins insisted that I stay longer, have a bite to eat with them, and see more of what they enthusiastically referred to as their *stuff,* a wonderful noun that is appreciated by collectors of every persuasion. "It's fun sharing it with people who love books," Lisa said of their library. "Most of the time when we're in here, we're by ourselves. We play."

The idea of perfectly sane adults "playing" with an assortment of curiosities might sound a bit odd, but it is, in my considered view, the ultimate reward a collector can receive for a job well done. Admittedly, there is a breed of collector who hoards material indiscriminately and squirrels it away without ever giving it another thought; for this person, the incentive is the chase itself, a thrilling adventure that has its denouement with a successful acquisition, and then the hunt is on for something else. More often than not, this person is what we call an *accumulator,* of whom the quintessential examples are Homer and Langley Collyer of New York City, two reclusive brothers who quite literally died under the collapsing weight of their various hoards in 1947, with one of them remaining buried for two and a half weeks before firefighters could locate his body beneath what was estimated to be 150 tons of newspapers, magazines, books, and assorted doodads. But their peculiar nature is not the focus of our attention here.

What I have seen in place after place is collectors who have assembled selections of materials that together create viable entities in their own right, and nothing gives them greater satisfaction than to share what they have accomplished with people who believe that books are not simply impersonal tools they use to acquire information, that they can be sources of satisfaction in and of themselves. Granted, there are some exceptions. Nobody, not the booksellers who sold him material, not even the two adult daughters who became his heirs, ever knew just how remarkable the American Indian collection put together by Dr. Frank T. Siebert was until he died in 1998 and it was consigned to Sotheby's for a two-part sale that realized $16 million the following year. Dr. Siebert's pleasure, apparently—and this is only speculation on the part of the few booksellers who had dealings with him—came with the assurance that what he had assembled in a remote house in Maine, and what he had learned from the materials, resulted in a major contribution to the understanding of Native American linguistic traditions, a corpus that is still being evaluated for its scholarship.

The overnight visit I made to the home of Rolland Comstock in the Missouri Ozarks involved a marathon run through two floors of books kept in a large library, the works of dead authors on the upper level, the works of the living below, with breaks taken only for cocktails, dinner, and a few hours of sleep. "It gets lonely out here in the mountains," Comstock said at one point, and when the three wolves he keeps on his property as pets began howling at the moon in the hours before daybreak, I had a deeper sense of what he meant. "That's the one problem I have with this collection," he said. "I have nobody around here I can show it to."

For Robert H. Jackson of Shaker Heights, Ohio, a prominent Cleveland attorney and arguably the most accomplished collector of Victorian novels in *parts,* or serials, on either side of the Atlantic, the great pleasure of collecting comes in reading the works the way they were intended by their authors to be read, one segment at a time, over measured periods of time. "I read everything I collect," Jackson told me. His other interests include the literature of travel; the Beat Generation with specific strength in the books, journals, and manuscripts of William Burroughs; a Southeast Asia manuscript collection "because I have been following the Silk Road on journeys with my wife"; a major collection of the illustrator Rockwell Kent "because I have always been fascinated by his travel"; and half a dozen other seemingly disparate collections that have as their only apparent point of convergence the overriding fact that Jackson finds them pleasing. "What ties all of these things together is my own curiosity," he made clear. "I have always been a curious person, I have always been a reader, and books lead me from area to area. I believe collecting is a desire for organization, and that you become a collector to satisfy yourself. Curiosity does not have to have a logic to it, you are curious about many things, but you do tend to gravitate to the areas that have particular fascination for you."

Jackson's serials collection numbers about three hundred Victorian novels. The most notable of these comprise the fiction of Charles Dickens (1812–1870), William Makepeace Thackeray (1811–1861), and Anthony Trollope (1815–1882), the vast majority of which were published in periodicals prior to their appearance in hard cover. "My motivation to collect them in parts was my fascination for the serial," Jackson said. "Usually, they would appear in twenty parts over a period of two years, and what I will do is read a part every day. The first readers would do this over two years; I do it over three to four weeks. What I realized after a while is that this particular collection is a series of stories within stories." Another interest that has grown out of the serials is what Jackson describes loosely as his "pre-1850 American novels in original boards and in the best possible condition that I can find" collection, focusing primarily on material that is "a cut below the high-priced trophy books" such as Herman Melville's *Moby-Dick* and Henry David Thoreau's *Walden.* "Those books are expensive and not terribly challenging because they are on everybody's list of important books. All you really need is the money to buy them. I have literature in my house just to educate me on these other people because I have never heard of most of them." Among the authors he is collecting in this category are such nineteenth-century American authors as Charles Brackton Brown, William G. Simms, and Lydia Marie Child. "I plan to give these books to the Library of Congress because they do not have many of these books in their original boards; what they have are rebound copies."

Active in the Cleveland arts community, Jackson and his wife, Donna, enjoy having writers and musicians stay in their home during visits to the area and showing off their collections. Two subjects of Jackson's collecting, the poet Allen Ginsberg and the writer William S. Burroughs, were both houseguests who saw firsthand what he was trying to accomplish with their literary creations. My introduction to the collections came in 1996 when I was in Ohio speaking to the Rowfant Club, a venerable book-collecting society in the city, which Jackson has served as president. "I am a great believer in mentoring," Jackson told me, a point he emphasized five years later in a speech he made at the Library of Congress, which was later published in the library's journal in 2002. "When I come across younger people who are really serious about collecting, I take them to shows in New York at the Pierpont Morgan Library and the New York Public Library, or over to Christie's and Sotheby's if there is a sale, and to give them an opportunity to absorb a bit of the ambiance. I like to walk through the whole process with them. Nobody ever collects the same things I collect, so it's a learning process for both of us; there's one young man who's a friend of my son, and who is now deeply into the history of lighter-than-air flying. I'm fascinated by what he's been able to assemble. We get together every two months or so, and the pleasure is that there is no competition between us. What I preach is looking for areas where you can collect *underneath* the obvious, areas where you can find good secondary material that others have ignored. My collection of pre-1850 American novels falls into that category."

By far one of the most unforgettable introductions I have ever had to a private collection came in November 2001 while I was in Florida taking part in the Miami Book Fair. A prominent Miami Beach couple came to my Sunday afternoon talk, introduced themselves, and invited me to their home that night for an immersion—that is my word, not theirs, but nothing else comes quite close to describing the experience—in what they confidently told me was the world's largest collection of "concrete and visual poetry," sixty-five thousand objects all told, a good many of them listed on the website for what is formally known as the Ruth and Marvin Sackner Archive of Concrete and Visual Poetry (www.rediscov.com/sackner). Formerly the director of internal medicine at Mount Sinai Medical Center in Miami, Dr. Sackner is now the head of a company that markets his various inventions, innovations such as a "suction catheter to remove secretions from the airways for people on mechanical ventilation," medical devices he continues to develop, he said, "because I need the income stream to finance our collecting habit"—and make no mistake, it is a habit. "Doing this collection is a full-time job," he said. "I have one major activity—my inventing—that exists for the purposes of supporting this full-time job."

What is significant in this context is just how thoroughly these objects have become a part of the Sackner household, a bonding of people and artifacts that is so seamless it was the subject of a chapter in *At Home with Books: How Booklovers Live with and Care for Their Libraries* (1995), a pioneering work by Estelle Ellis, Caroline Seebohm, and Christopher Simon Sykes, which is notable for some exceptional photographs of people and their collections. "We began by buying pictures that had *words* in them," Ruth Sackner said, explaining how one of the most unusual book collections I have ever seen anywhere—books in every manner of shape, substance, and form—got started from a modern art collection begun in the early 1970s. She agreed that the enthusiasm she and her husband have for the material as a couple is undoubtedly responsible for the explosive growth of the collection over the years. "I don't think you could say that one of us loves this material any more than the other."

During a visit to southern California in the fall of 2001, my wife and I were dazzled by how intelligently and decisively the Americana collection put together by Louise Taper of Beverly Hills had progressed since the last time we had seen it a full decade earlier, and by the exciting new directions it had taken. When we first met in 1991, Taper's consuming passion for all things concerned with Abraham Lincoln had already put her in position to claim distinction as the Lincoln collector by whom all others, past and present, would have to be measured.

On that visit, she had shown us an extraordinary variety of books, letters, documents, and artifacts pertaining not only to Lincoln's life and presidency, but also to the lives of his ancestors, the family of his wife, Mary Todd Lincoln, and the theatrical family of the assassin John Wilkes Booth. In 1993, selections of Taper's collection would form the centerpiece of an exhibition at the Huntington Library in nearby San Marino that drew three hundred thousand visitors, a heady achievement for one determined collector, but still just a work-in-progress, as we saw when we visited her home eight years later. Now there was a huge bronze bust of Lincoln to admire in the courtyard, along with recently acquired pieces of presidential china from various administrations on display in several glass cases, hats worn by numerous chief executives in another, including a stovepipe by Lincoln, a fedora by Dwight D. Eisenhower, a baseball cap by Bill Clinton, and an entirely new area of interest—unpublished proof sheets of photographs taken of Marilyn Monroe with Carl Sandburg, the poet and biographer of Lincoln, by Arnold Newman—being catalogued in her study. As Taper walked us around from area to area in the house, each containing an astounding gathering of presidential objects—"Lincoln's DNA is all over the place," she said at one point, indicating the shirt the sixteenth president was wearing on the night he was shot, and some locks of his hair—the fire and confidence of a scholar at work was apparent in every word she spoke, fully involved in every object, its significance as an artifact, its relationship to the whole. But there also was a laugh to share. "Did you notice how the people who don't collect started to bail out after dinner when it came time to look at the collection?" she asked toward the end of the evening. "It happens all the time." As for where the collection goes next, she shrugged. "The fun of it all is not knowing where it's headed," she said. "It's knowing that there will be more surprises."

In a suburb of Rochester, New York, a visit to the house of Dr. Seymour I. Schwartz, formerly the head of surgery at the University of Rochester Medical Center, gave us an opportunity to see in room after room an array of historical maps and charts that document, in one sweeping panorama, the discovery, exploration, and settlement of North America. A prolific author of medical texts and articles who has served as editor in chief of the *Journal of the American College of Surgeons,* Dr. Schwartz told us he began a cartographic collection in midcareer at the behest of his late wife, also a physician, "who told me I was too intensely monolithic a person and that I needed to broaden my interests." So, to lighten up the load, he chose maps, and it wasn't long before he was writing authoritatively about his hobby, numbering among his accomplishments several highly regarded illustrated books based on the materials assembled so tastefully in his house, *The Mapping of America* (1980), *The French and Indian War 1754–1763: The Imperial Struggle for North America* (1994), and *This Land Is Your Land: The Geographic Evolution of the United States* (2000) among them.

Our trip to Rochester included another unscheduled visit, this one with John Topham, a transplanted Southerner from Virginia who made a career as a consultant in building construction. Topham's great claim to collecting-fame came from a diversion he pursued relentlessly while living in Saudi Arabia during the mid-1970s overseeing a major project that had been suffering "serious schedule trouble." While there, the lifelong collector of "everything interesting" began gathering Bedouin tapestries from all sections of the country, a collection of five hundred specimens so comprehensive that it was more sophisticated than anything preserved in the country itself. In an effort to document the collection, Topham assembled a library of thirteen hundred books dealing with the region and its traditions. His 1982 monograph, *Traditional Crafts of Saudi Arabia,* occasioned a touring exhibition sponsored by the Smithsonian Institution and a request from the wife of the Saudi ambassador to the United States that he sell the collection to her, with the understanding that it ultimately would go on permanent display in Saudi Arabia. "I agreed," Topham told us over bowls of sorrel soup that he had made from herbs grown in his garden, "but like everything else I've sold or given away, I dearly wish I had it all back here with me." What remained behind in his house, however, was amazing enough to see, and to describe it all properly—maps of New York state, engravings of the nearby Genesse Falls, engravings (in the "choo-choo" room) of locomotives, 350 nineteenth-century cigar holders in the basement, shelf upon shelf of travel literature, various weavings, all sorts of Americana—would take up a chapter in its own right.

I am constantly reminded in these wanderings of Anthony Powell's comic novel of 1971 with the delightful title, *Books Do Furnish a Room,* and how such a cozy premise is incorporated into the lives of so many people who combine their deep interest in books with enhancements that lend themselves so agreeably to display. All three floors of the Chicago condominium apartment of Dr. C. Frederick Kittle and his wife, Ann, including the stairways, boast original paintings by five members of the immediate family of Arthur Conan Doyle, each of whom was an accomplished artist, and numerous period posters related to the works of the master. What Dr. Kittle calls the Kittle Collection of Doyleana began in the 1950s when one medical professional—Dr. Kittle—became interested in the writings of another, as the creator of Sherlock Holmes, it happens, was a practicing physician. "My first acquisition was the original manuscript of Doyle's *Romance of Medicine,* a nineteen-page, handwritten medical lecture he gave at St. Mary's Hospital Medical School in London," Dr. Kittle said. As his interest in the subject grew, so too did the scope of the collection, with a particular focus on everything he could locate *around* the Holmes corpus of works, though that came well within his purview too, as the fourteen original manuscripts, including the author's holograph text for *The White Company,* readily attest. Beyond the comfort this material provides around the house comes the additional pleasure of benefaction, as the Kittles have decided to donate their entire collection to the Newberry Library in Chicago, giving the institution, in an instant, a research archive of international stature. Because theme collections tend to be driven by a particular passion, they have a way of arousing a plethora of emotions. Some, like the Literature of AIDS books I discussed in chapter 5, contain the power to provoke moods of profound concern and contemplation, even unease, in the beholder. At the other extreme entirely are what I like to think of as "feel good" collections, gatherings that come into being for the simple reason that they allow their creators an opportunity to derive uncomplicated joy from what they have put together. By far the most moving example of this genre to my experience are the 3,500 yuletide objects assembled by Jock Elliott, chairman emeritus of the New York advertising company Ogilvy & Mather, and the subject of an exhibition of 150 selected highlights at the Grolier Club in 1999 that drew hundreds of admiring visitors. Dazzled by the depth of the collection then, and totally charmed by the lovely illustrated catalog Elliott wrote to accompany it, I leaped at the invitation he extended in the spring of 2002 to give my wife and me a guided introduction to the treasures he had assembled in situ at Highland Fling, his country house in Westchester County.

The most obvious question for me, and I asked it

straightaway, was why Christmas and not something else? "Why not?" Elliott countered amiably as he was laying out several of the eight first edition copies of Charles Dickens's *A Christmas Carol* he owns, each one slightly different from the other, particularly in the color of the endpapers, a matter of some bibliographical consequence, since Dickens was notorious for nitpicking every element of the publishing process for this book. "Dickens had the title page printed in red and green with green endpapers to match, because those are cheery colors," Elliott said. "But when he found that the green began to smudge, he switched to red and blue title pages and yellow endpapers." We saw other examples of authorial tinkering for this timeless story, and there were numerous additional curiosities for us to ponder, including the first mention of *A Christmas Carol* in print, a tiny notice buried on the last page of the November 25, 1843, issue of the London newspaper *Britannia*. "As an advertising man, I have to laugh every time I take a look at this," Elliott said. "No hype at all, just this modest little announcement, and you get one of the great best-sellers of all time."

Elliott is a cheerful man who began collecting these materials in 1983 following his retirement from the advertising business. "I had always collected a variety of different things, but before I got serious with Christmas, my style was pretty much hit-or-miss," he said. In the introduction to his catalog, titled *A Ha! Christmas* (The Grolier Club of New York, 1999), Elliott wrote how his passion for the festive holiday began early in life. "My childhood Christmases were magical, made so by both my parents, but particularly my mother," and it is that image that has constantly defined his focus. Favoring the secular aspect of the holiday, Elliott bought impulsively at first, with acquisitions that ranged from "near junk" to unique rarity. Before long he had set his sights on what was precious and important, and a pattern emerged that stressed the acquisition of "firsts." Included in his collection, for instance, are the first-known illustration of a Christmas tree (1835); the first illustration of St. Nicholas by Thomas Nast (1863); a copy of *The Golden Legend* printed by William Caxton (1483), comprising the first account in English of the story of the birth of Christ; a first printing of John Milton's *Hymn on the Morning of Christ's Nativity* (1645); and the first Christmas card to be produced commercially (1843). Other "firsts" include the first printed illustration of Santa Claus descending a chimney (1841) and a copy of *An Itinerary* (1617), a travel book written by Fynes Morysen Gent, in which the words "Merry" and "Christmas" appear together for the first time.

Elliott's collection boasts numerous broadsides and original art, a number of which decorate his library. The shelves, meanwhile, shimmer with appealing titles, with pertinent works by such luminaries as William Makepeace Thackeray, Hans Christian Anderson, Wilkie Collins, Horatio Alger, and W. Somerset Maugham sparkling brightly among them. His favorite piece of prose is *A Child's Christmas in Wales* by Dylan Thomas; his favorite poem is Edna St. Vincent Millay's *The Ballad of the Harp-Weaver,* the heartbreaking story in verse of a penniless mother whose unconditional love for a child concludes with the woman's death, a poignant work that won a Pulitzer Prize in 1923. Elliott said he reads the narrative poem aloud to his wife, Eleanor, every Christmas Eve, an exercise that unfailingly brings tears to their eyes. The Elliotts have no children, but that circumstance does not stop them from hanging a huge red stocking above the fireplace and filling it with gifts that are opened at the crack of dawn on Christmas Day. An embroidered pillow on a divan says it all: "I believe in Santa Claus."

As this touching tableau makes clear, Jock Elliott's collection is a living entity that provides continual sustenance. Very often there will be an instance in which a collector determines that the material is not providing the kind of creature comfort it once did, and that it is time to bid it adieu. A few years before he died in 1992, Carl Petersen of St. Louis, Missouri, sold a magnificent collection of William Faulkner material to Peter B. Howard, owner of Serendipity Books of Berkeley, California, for $445,000. Always a man of modest means, Petersen acknowledged in his discussions with me that money very definitely was a factor in his decision, especially as he approached retirement, but the clincher came when he realized just how valuable his holdings were, and that he could no longer enjoy them as he had in the past. "The major items in the collection—the *Marble Faun* typescript, for instance—were all in a bank vault, all out of sight. So what was I supposed to do, go down to the bank once a week and play with them? I never got bored with the collection, but once the decision was made, I had no problems living with it."

Following a somewhat different tack, Victor Gulotta of Newton, Massachusetts, a prominent literary publicist who became deeply involved in the search for every manner of item relating to the life and career of Henry Wadsworth Longfellow (1807–1882) during the late-1980s, found a willing suitor at the Houghton Library of Harvard University, repository of the richest archive of material relating to

the nineteenth-century New England poet to be found anywhere, including extensive holdings of literary manuscripts
and material transferred over in 1976 by the trustees of the
Longfellow House Trust. Making the sale of considerable
consequence to private collectors and the scholarly community alike—and the price was said to be in the "middle six figures"—was the fact that Gulotta had concentrated his efforts
on what researchers from another era might consider primary material of peripheral interest, the sort of object I have
been describing in these pages as *enhancements* to the traditional book collection, and that provide one of the most
exciting opportunities, in my view, to the book hunter of the
twenty-first century. Especially instructive, too, is the fact
that Gulotta chose to concentrate on a poet whose charming
but dated verses had fallen out of fashion in recent years, and
whose books as a consequence could be had for a fraction of
what they once commanded in the antiquarian market.

There most assuredly were books in Gulotta's collection,
all of the first editions, in fact, and a number of them quite
important for their associations, but little in and of themselves
that would entice Harvard—which has copies of everything
Longfellow produced in abundance—to react so enthusiastically at the prospect of acquiring what he had gathered. What
pleased the university more than anything when it bought the
material in July 2001, according to William P. Stoneman, the
Florence Fearrington Librarian of Houghton Library, were
"material artifacts" such as photographs, dozens of letters in
Longfellow's hand, nineteenth-century dishes bearing verses
from his best-known narrative poems, labels for Longfellow
beer, packages of commemorative cigarettes and cigars from
the 1920s, busts, posters, calendars, engravings, lithographs,

more than a thousand objects all told, that "fill gaps" in the university's collection.

"Scholars today are interested not only in how literary and historical works are created by their original authors, but also how they were received by their first readers and disseminated to various audiences over time," Stoneman told me. "This is the reason that we have collections of the manuscripts and papers of authors and first editions, but also annotated copies and subsequent editions. Sequels, parodies, adaptations also demonstrate the reputation and influence of the original work. So do other material artifacts such as dust jackets, medals, busts, photographs, and figurines. The raw materials of scholarship can take many forms, and often these artifacts can make a point more effectively in an exhibition, for example, than words reported in a letter or a book."

Gulotta very definitely did "strut" his stuff, and contentedly so; he filled his house with the material and reveled in showing it to visitors. But he also felt that it was time to let it go, particularly since a major research library had expressed such interest in acquiring it. "One of the reasons I was able to do this so successfully is because Longfellow was no longer the darling of the collectors," he admitted, noting that it was a teacher of his at the State University of New York, Buffalo, in the 1970s, the poet Robert Creeley, who "helped me appreciate some of the great nineteenth-century American poets and their lives." Once he realized that so much material, including a good deal of what is called *realia,* was available—and at very reasonable prices, given the paucity of demand—Gulotta became obsessed with the quest. "I made a point of tracking down any significant or uncommon Longfellow items I could find. My sources were bookstores, book- and autograph-dealer catalogs, the Internet, auctions, fairs, and private collectors."

Gulotta admitted that he felt a bit of "separation anxiety" once the material had left his house, but at forty-seven years of age, he figured he still had new worlds to conquer, and the resources now to elevate, perhaps, the level of his activity. "Now that I'm no longer laser-focused on one author—for which I have no regrets whatsoever—I have the freedom to be a dilettante."

CHAPTER 10

02-02-02:
A DAY AT THE FAIR

Of the scores of itinerant book bazaars mounted throughout the United States each year, the lively festival held on the West Coast the first weekend in February is the largest in the country, larger even than the New York Antiquarian Book Fair held every April in the Seventh Regiment Armory on Park Avenue. What helps make it one of the most exciting to attend is that it alternates year to year between Los Angeles and San Francisco, with its return engagement in each city an event to anticipate among local bibliophiles. By pure chance it happened that the second day of the Thirty-fifth California International Book Fair fell on February 2, 2002, an appealing detail for someone about to sign copies of a new book for three and a half hours and keen on having something of interest to include in the inscriptions. Some 280 booksellers from all over North America, and a good number from abroad, had brought their wares to Los Angeles for the three-day event, providing an unequaled opportunity for visitors to see a striking variety of fresh material assembled under one roof while seizing an opportunity to meet new dealers, grab up descriptive catalogs to their heart's content, and get acquainted with other collectors. At the formal opening the night before, the line to get inside had snaked its way around the long lobby outside the ballroom of the Los Angeles Airport Marriott Hotel all the way back to the escalator. It quickly became apparent that people had come to buy, not just browse.

Outside the main entrance to the exhibition, a table had been set up where I would spend the better part of two days signing copies of my books. Regarded by some authors as a tedious exercise, this is something I enjoy doing, especially when most of the people I meet are likely to be people with stories to share about their adventures in the hunt for books. Normally I use roman numerals to record the dates in my inscriptions, but when I saw the *Los Angeles Times* that morning taking note of the unusual gathering of identical numbers, I knew instantly that I was on to something special, so instead of writing II. II. MMII underneath my signature as I otherwise would have, I decided instead to go with 02-02-02, a novelty that everybody there seemed to appreciate.

One of the first people waiting in line for an inscription described his collecting interests as Charles Darwin and the history of evolution; as I was writing something appropriate in his book, he added, almost as an afterthought, "and I have thirteen tons of newspapers." I looked up with a questioning glance, and he didn't miss a beat: "The London *Times*," Garrett Herman said: "1809 to 1882, about sixty thousand issues all told, and all bound." Supposedly, that should have been a sufficient explanation for me, but my continued puzzlement prompted the following embellishment: "What I have is every day of Darwin's life." I would later learn that Herman, a Toronto investment banker, acquired the run in 1996 from the Law Society of Upper Canada, which like so many other institutional libraries around the world, had turned to microfilmed copies of newspapers to save space, and opted to discard the cumbersome originals, a disquieting practice that is at the heart of Nicholson Baker's 2001 book on preservation policies, *Double Fold*. Once Herman renovated the basement in his Victorian house to shelve the massive trove, the total cost was about one hundred thousand dollars. The good news is that most of the newspapers in the collection were printed on rag paper—the era of acidic wood pulp began in earnest in the 1870s—making his hoard all the more likely to survive for generations to come. Altogether a fantastic undertaking, I thought instantly, one full of verve, panache, and originality.

Presently, a man named Joel Stern came by with a snapshot description of his activity. "I love origami and pop-ups," he said, confiding that he has something like five hundred "intervisual" and "movable" books in his collection, a few going back to the 1800s, including several made by the German masters Ernest Nister and Lothar Meggendorfer, an interest inspired by his having dabbled as a "paper engineer" for a company that makes books notable for their revolving parts and movable flaps.

Before long, a professional book scout from Australia who described herself as a "perennial hanger-outer in thrift stores and yard sales," and "blessed with a knack for finding things for peanuts that I can sell to dealers for fifty dollars," stepped up to the table. Her collecting specialty? "Gypsies," she said.

"I am descended from a gypsy family that settled in Wales before moving Down Under. I learned to read when I was two years old; my parents bought a house that was what we call a 'deceased estate,' meaning it came with contents, including a marvelously stocked library." Shortly thereafter a young man named Stuart Moore, a collector of books written by winners of the Nobel Prize for literature during his lifetime, came by, and he was particularly taken by 02-02-02, noting that he was born on November 11, 1966, creating a combination of 11-11-66. "I like numbers a lot," he said, and my feeling was that this was an area that could be a fascinating collecting interest in its own right.

Children's books are very popular among collectors, and at a signing I can always count on making the acquaintance of someone who claims this as a specialty. One woman at the Los Angeles fair confided that she was collecting primarily for her own youngsters, not so much for herself, and the inscription she asked for in her copy of my book was to her daughters. Signing books for young readers is always a treat for me—who says that print is a moribund medium?—and I responded with a lengthy, hopeful inscription. I had another collector stop by whose interest was in the history of magic and conjuring, and yet another who asked me to pen in a quotation that he identified as from Alexander Pope's *Essay on Man*, "What can we know, but from what we read."

As the afternoon drew to a close, a retired bookseller from Ensino, California, came by, and with the traffic having slowed down considerably by this time, we chatted a bit about his experiences in the trade. The man identified himself as John Makarewich, eighty-one years old and still an enthusiastic collector of materials relating to a lifelong interest in the martial arts. "I moved out here from Michigan in the 1940s," he said, having decided at an early age that there was a future to pursue as a bookseller. "When I was ten years old I bought a copy of *Tarzan of the Apes* with a great dust jacket on it for a nickel at the Salvation Army store in East Detroit, and I sold it a couple days later to a bookseller for a quarter. He then sold it for a dollar to somebody else who wanted a copy in nice condition. That was terrific money during the Depression, and I didn't have to be a genius to figure out that this was a pretty good way for somebody to make a living."

Everything is relative, needless to say, and the numbers have changed geometrically—a nicely jacketed copy of Edgar Rice Burroughs's *Tarzan of the Apes* (1914) was being offered just inside the hall for $50,000—but the principle outlined by Makarewich, supply and demand, hasn't changed much over the years, as I was reminded soon enough when my signing session was over and I had a chance to spend some time browsing about the various booths and talking shop with the dealers. As much as they want to sell their inventory, booksellers will tell you that buying fresh stock from each other is just as attractive an incentive, and probably the number one reason why major book fairs are in no great danger of expiring any time soon, though everyone I spoke to readily acknowledged that some of the smaller events are likely to disappear under continued pressure from the Internet. "I would estimate that seventy-five to eighty percent of the money that changes hands at a book fair is among dealers," Louis Weinstein, founder in 1963 with his brother Ben of Heritage Book Store, told me a few days before the fair opened. When I saw Weinstein at an elegant party he hosted at his store on Saturday night, he confided that he had spent $250,000 on eight books before the fair had opened its doors to the public.

That Los Angeles is home to the film colony is a reality not lost on the dealers who always try to target material to the local market. A fine copy of *The Maltese Falcon* (1930) inscribed by Dashiell Hammett, the author, for instance, was featured front and center at one booth for $110,000. With the newly released blockbuster films *Harry Potter and the Sorcerer's Stone* and *Lord of the Rings* fresh in everyone's mind, assorted J. K. Rowling and J. R. R. Tolkien titles were available in abundance, all of them listed at substantial prices, in some instances reflecting figures recorded at recent auctions, while in others farther "off the scale" altogether. Attracting the most comment by far on these "flavor of the month" titles—the "high spots of the moment," according to one stage whisper—was the $140,000 being asked by Bertram Rota Ltd. of London for signed copies of *The Hobbit* (1937), *The Fellowship of the Ring* (1954), *The Two Towers* (1954), *The Return of the King* (1955), and *Adventures of Tom Bombadil* (1962), all nicely jacketed but not all first issues, though each was signed by Tolkien, and two letters in the author's hand were being included as a bonus. The interest in all things Tolkien had prompted David Brass, a fourth-generation British bookseller now working in Los Angeles with the Weinsteins at Hertitage Books as executive vice president, and highly regarded for his intimate knowledge of the trade, to tell in the *Los Angeles Times* how delighted he and his colleagues would be "if Hollywood would make a fifteen-part miniseries of John Galsworthy," the idea being that the no-longer-hot-as-a-pistol works of the

1932 Nobel Prize winner could reclaim a fraction of the market value they once enjoyed.

But it was the changing nature of the business itself, not the ups and downs of certain authors, that seemed to be on the minds of the dealers I talked with in a series of impromptu interviews I found myself conducting at booth after booth. Given the enthusiasm that some collectors were showing in their rush for all things Tolkien and Rowling, I was taken by the offerings of Ralph Sipper of Santa Barbara, California. The founder and former president of Joseph the Provider Books—and known forever after as "Joe the Pro"—Sipper has always impressed me as an astute observer of the book business and always candid in discussing its vicissitudes. For this fair, he had brought in a selection of titles he called "good books made into good movies," as arbitrary a listing as you could imagine on the subject, but one that clearly reflects *his* point of view, and is very much a collection-in-progress.

Instead of highlighting the usual suspects—James Jones's *From Here to Eternity,* Mario Puzo's *The Godfather,* Harper Lee's *To Kill a Mockingbird,* or Margaret Mitchell's *Gone with the Wind,* for instance, although those are certainly highly desirable acquisitions in the genre, and by no means to be dismissed—Sipper has been concentrating on some lesser-known works of fiction that were the basis of productions he believes are equally as important, films such as Sergio Leone's 1984 production of *Once upon a Time in America* starring Robert De Niro, James Woods, and Elizabeth McGovern, and based on Harry Grey's 1952 novel, *The Hoods.* Other titles on Sipper's list include Raymond Chandler's *The Big Sleep* (1939), C. S. Forester's *The African Queen*

(1935), and B. Traven's *The Treasure of the Sierra Madre* (1935). Sipper said that he began assembling the collection about fifteen years ago, and that the finest books will remain together as a unit until he has completed the project, at which time he probably will offer them for sale en bloc. Books he brought to the Los Angeles fair were either duplicates, or titles he had "winnowed" out of an original list of four hundred titles. "I could have gone to a thousand easily, but when it gets that large, the overall quality tends to get diluted. So what I have decided is that in order to qualify for this collection, a book has to be something that is collected as a literary work in its own right, the copies themselves have to be in 'Joe the Pro' condition, and I want the adaptation that came out of it also to be a film of indisputable quality."

To make the collection special—to enhance the value of the individual objects, essentially—Sipper said that he upgrades "until I get the very best copies I can find," and that he constantly seeks out ways "to make each one a *better* copy"— the German dealer in illuminated manuscripts Heribert Tenschert would call them *prime* copies—"by laying something significant inside." Thus, to make the copy of Jack Schaefer's 1949 Western novel, *Shane,* really special, Sipper located a signed photograph of the actor Alan Ladd, pictured "in character" for the lead role; for the fine copy of Robert Penn Warren's 1946 masterpiece, *All the King's Men,* Sipper acquired and laid in the contract Broderick Crawford had signed to play the role of Willy Stark in the 1950 adaptation, a performance that earned him an Academy Award for best actor. Just a few hours before we spoke, Sipper had bought from another dealer a copy of *A Clockwork Orange* (1962), inscribed by the author, Anthony Burgess, to his personal physician. Of the books Sipper had "winnowed" out and brought along to the Los Angeles fair, he wound up selling about seventy-five, including a copy of J. B. Priestley's 1927 Gothic novel, *Benighted*, which was the inspiration for the 1932 horror-comedy, *The Old Dark House*, featuring Boris Karloff in his first starring role, and showcasing the talents of a stunning young starlet named Gloria Stuart, who made a triumphant appearance in full maturity sixty-five years later in *Titanic*.

For all the razmatazz of Hollywood and the material that nourishes its industry, Sipper was most ebullient about his purchase that Saturday of what he called the "black tulip of modern drug literature," a novel titled *Dope Darling: A Story of Cocaine*, written under a pseudonym by David Garnett (Leda Burke), a member of the legendary Bloomsbury group in London, and published in 1919 in an obscure paperback edition. "I first learned about this book twenty-five years ago when I was in England, and I have been looking for a copy ever since," Sipper said, showing me the prize, which he had just priced for resale at $18,500. "There are only two known examples of this book in institutional collections, one at the British Library, the other at Yale. Very few people know what it is—and today, in this ballroom, I found this copy, which, as you can see, is in remarkably fine condition."

That a bookseller should be more excited about his purchases than his sales might sound a bit odd, but finding fresh material is the high-octane fuel that keeps these fairs firing away on all cylinders. "The way to figure out whether or not you've had a good fair is to add the sum of your sales to the sum of your purchases," Tom Congalton, the owner of Between the Covers of Merchantville, New Jersey, told me.

"Just about every dealer I know spends $100,000 or more on books at a big fair like this, which is a lot more than you can say for most of your customers. So a fair with a lot of book-sellers on the prowl is like a room full of well-heeled customers. My philosophy is that if you can't sell your way out of one of these things, you buy your way out. A third corollary is if you can't buy your way out, then you drink your way out, but that's another story altogether."

Congalton distributes some of the more attractive dealer catalogs issued in recent years, illustrating every book he lists with a color photograph of the dust jacket. For Valentine's Day, he issued a list of 255 "romance books," basically a selection of light novels from the first third of the twentieth century drawn from a pool of about 700 books Congalton has gathered over several decades, all reasonably priced, and all largely forgotten, with titles ranging from Frank Walker Allen's *The Lovers of Skye* (1913) and Eleanor Blake's *Wherever I Choose* (1938), to Basil King's *Satan as Lightning* (1929) and Pamela Wynne's *Ashes of Desire* (1930). The enduring value of a catalog like this, especially since it reproduces the cover art, is the documentation it provides of books that have largely disappeared from institutional collections, having been discarded over the years as either out of fashion or lacking in social value.

Two booksellers who specialize in American fiction of the twentieth century, Peter Stern of Boston and Jeffrey Marks of Rochester, New York, work together on a number of projects, and regularly show their wares at book fairs, regardless of the turnouts. "I've done hundreds and hundreds of these things," Stern said, "and I can honestly say that we still really don't know what we're doing. All we really know is what we've *done*. I know the books that I've sold, and the prices they've realized, but I have no idea what the future holds." Unlike most of his colleagues, Marks, also a practicing attorney, refuses to post on the Internet his literary first editions, which include some truly magnificent copies of the works of William Faulkner, F. Scott Fitzgerald, and Ernest Hemingway at premium prices, and he does not maintain a website. "It may sound old-fashioned to say so, but I like to know where my books are going; the day this ceases to be a hands-on business is the day I close it down and practice law full-time. The thing of it is, I have no desire to know everything there is to know in the world at any given time. I still like going into a store."

Of course for every dealer who is buying at a fair, there is another dealer selling, and for Allen and Patricia Ahearn, owners of Quill & Brush of Dexter, Maryland, pay dirt occurred before the first collector had entered the grand ballroom. "We made the nut," Allen Ahearn told me with a broad smile, and by that he explained that the trip across the continent had already been covered by his sale to another dealer for $95,000 of the first issue copy of Walt Whitman's *Leaves of Grass* he had just acquired a couple weeks earlier.

Without exception, every dealer I talked to was alert to changes taking place in the profession and all too willing to offer a thought or two about what is going on, particularly with how the Internet is changing the way they do business. The most obvious development, they all agreed, has been an almost herdlike interest in "high spot" collecting, an impatient need among so many to have the very best there is, and to have it right now. Don Reisler of Vienna, Virginia, with his wife, Jo Ann, a dealer in fine children's books and fairy tales, said he sees some significant changes in what people are looking for as collectors. "My sense is that people today are less likely to follow their instincts. They're more interested in what's proven, what's certified. I guess the collectors I admire the most are the collectors who have the courage to believe in their own taste."

I mentioned to John Windle of San Francisco—a native of England who began his career as a bookseller with Quaritch of London and worked with the late Warren Howell before opening his own shop specializing in medieval manuscripts and illustrated books from the fifteenth to the nineteenth centuries—a theory put forth by Allan Stypeck, the owner of Second Story Books in Washington, D.C., proposing a "five Ds" principle to explain the different ways fresh material, once thought to be out of circulation, suddenly comes back on the market. "Death, Disinterest, Divorce, Displacement, and Debt," Stypeck had offered on one of the nationally syndicated *Book Guys* radio shows he hosts every week, and on which I appear regularly as a guest. "This is how a bookseller gets books today. Write those words down and think about them. They need no elaboration."

Windle smiled at the premise, and said he has a theory of his own involving a number of those categories to explain how important material has a way of getting back into circulation, his dealing with what he called a "three-year window" involving the sale of books to beginners of considerable means who decide, in the flush of newly made fortunes, to collect books. "My theory says that there is a window of opportunity with high-end collectors that the astute bookseller is wise to exploit," Windle said. "We are talking quite specifically here about very wealthy people who are looking for ways to spend their money. In a nutshell, what happens is that they come into the trade, they catch fire, and then they burn out, all in three years. Why do they stop? They stop because they run out of things that are easy for them to get, and they run out of patience. Their attention spans are short. They will come to a fair like this, they will go to the big-name dealers, they buy the big books, they write a fat check. We *know* who most of these people are, by the way. You hear a name, you look it up, it says 'So-and-so, partner in Goldman Sachs,' that sort of thing. When these guys are in full blaze, they will buy anything, and they don't ask the price. That is the time you must act. You show them the books they *ought* to have, and they will write you a check on the spot."

When the three years are up, Windle continued, "the books go and sit on the shelves where they are forgotten *until* the divorce comes along." Then, one of two things happens. "Either the books become a bitter issue of contention in the matter of the settlement, or somehow they go unnoticed, and in that case the trophy wife finds out what they are worth, and *she* sends them off to Christie's." The "true collector," in Windle's estimation, "is the person who gets interested *after* he's got all the obvious books he is told by experts like myself that he *ought* to have. This is the person who asks, 'Where are the manuscripts? Do we have any letters? Where are the drawings? Where are the proofs? *Teach* me something I don't know.' *That* is the person you want to cultivate. *That* is the person I am interested in helping."

A person who would qualify as an *ideal* collector by this paradigm is the late Sanford L. Berger of Carmel, California, whose remarkable archive of materials relating to the life and work of the British poet, designer, and bookmaker William

Morris went to the Huntington Library in California in 2000 after a protracted round of negotiations conducted among a number of institutional suitors. Berger had insisted in his interviews with me that wherever his collection went—and in addition to everything produced by Morris's Kelmscott Press, it included textiles, wallpaper, carpets, tapestries, stained glass, pottery, drawings, watercolors, journals, company records, workbooks, Utopian socialist writings by Morris and his associates—everything "be kept in one place," and while the amount of money was a factor in the talks, it was not the deciding issue. In fact Berger was reported in the press to have offered the collection to the Victoria & Albert Museum in London at a 25 percent discount off the appraised value of $5 million—the price he is believed to have finally received from the Huntington—if guarantees along those lines could be made. It was Berger, incidentally, who described for me the way he felt after acquiring his first Kelmscott Press book as suffering from "a severe case of anticipation syndrome," a condition that went away only after he bought the other fifty books that he needed to fill out that magnificent run of fine-press books.

Berger, who died not long after the sale to the Huntington was consummated, was a "hands-on" kind of person who insisted on doing most of the negotiations himself, and it was only when Windle was invited in to represent his interests that a successful solution could be reached. "Sandy was the most extraordinary completist I have ever seen," Windle said, "and his one flaw so far as I can determine was that he tried to do it all on his own. I believe it is a mistake for an individual to try and sell a collection of that magnitude all by himself. The purchasers don't like it because the collector unfailingly has an inaccurate sense of the value; it's either impossibly high, or if the collection was put together at a time when prices were not nearly what they are today, it's much too low. But it's never in the middle where it ought to be. Sandy's problem came when he tried to sell the collection to these institutions on his own, and there was, as you know, a lot of baggage in the way of certain requirements he was demanding. Institutions prefer dealing with an agent because there is no legal recourse with an individual the way there is with a professional, for one thing, but also because it makes for a much cleaner and much more equitable resolution."

I was pleased during this trip to the West Coast by the opportunity I had to spend some time with Lou Weinstein, not only at various points on that Saturday, but a few nights earlier when we appeared together on a local television program to promote the fair, and over a leisurely dinner of chicken pot pie and fine wine at Musso & Frank Grill, the oldest restaurant in Hollywood, and once the haunt of F. Scott Fitzgerald, John O'Hara, Dashiell Hammett, Dorothy Parker, William Faulkner, and Raymond Chandler. Of the many success stories in the antiquarian book business, Weinstein has followed a career path that is uniquely his own, starting out in 1963 with his brother Ben as the owners of a small business buying and selling assorted secondhand books, becoming in due course the highest-grossing antiquarian book business in the United States, with annual sales said to be routinely in eight figures. What is most remarkable about Weinstein is his no-nonsense approach; he readily admits that everything he knows about the business he learned through trial and error, and when there is something he doesn't know, he isn't ashamed to hire someone with the expertise to provide it. "I have good people writing my catalogs, good people in every department," he said. "I do my job, and I pay them well to do theirs."

Unlike most of his colleagues who say that buying, not selling, is the most arduous task a bookseller faces, Weinstein finds the greater challenge in "negotiating" for new stock, a fine distinction involving many of the same skills, to be sure, but this is a businessman who is operating in the twenty-first century under twenty-first-century rules, and numerous nuances frequently do come to the fore. Ask Weinstein what his specialty is, and he replies that he specializes in "anything that is good," with a subtle refinement: "I am not fussy in that I will deal in *anything* of unusual value. I am interested in the high-end material. Why? Because I would much rather sell one book for ten thousand dollars than a hundred books at one hundred dollars each."

While he admittedly prefers the glamorous titles to offer his customers in nearby Beverly Hills and Bel Air, Weinstein carries a full selection of material, and it is at the lower end of the scale where the Internet earns its keep. "The printed catalogs are absolutely necessary; they are expensive to produce, but you need them if only for the sake of maintaining your credibility. Anyone ordering from you for the first time will not buy a book over the Internet of more than a few thousand dollars, you have to earn their trust, and like every other kind of business, collectors have to be cultivated with great care. Most collectors tend to gravitate toward what the booksellers have to offer them at any particular time, and from my experience it is the bookseller who seems to shape taste in the market. What we have in stock tends to define in many cases what people are going to collect. I'm not saying that's a good thing or a bad thing, I'm just saying that's the way it is."

On the advisability of buying certified high spots, Weinstein said he believes "they are the safest place to put your money, believe it or not, because every year silly prices just keep getting sillier and sillier. One thing you can definitely say about the Internet is that people have become intensely aware of just how *common* obscure books are. They're all over the place. With regard to modern books, I compare them to the dot-com companies. Who can tell what's going to happen with something that's only been around for a little while? When people ask me about the hypermoderns, I tell them they're paying too much money, period. When somebody spends a couple thousand dollars today on something that's just been published, they should be cognizant of the fact that this is not an item that will ever represent *real* value, because there is no *real* scarcity. More often than not it is a temporary phenomenon, and chances are that it will never be a *rare* book. But the remarkable nature of this business is that you can never really be sure about anything."

Truer words were never spoken, as my wife and I found out soon enough on the night of 02-02-02 when we arrived at the Heritage Book Shop on 8540 Melrose Avenue for the lovely dinner party Lou and Ben Weinstein had laid on for the booksellers assembled in Los Angeles. Weinstein is always doing business, even when he's entertaining, and his staff were busy showing off choice wares to his guests, some of them were writing up invoices, others were wrapping up merchandise. Weinstein had joked the day before that one sure method he has developed over the years for finding fresh stock is to arrive early at a fair and offer to help other dealers unpack their inventory and set up their shelves, a practice he said he continues to this day. Before long we made our way to a spacious room on the second floor that sparkled with original paintings, a veritable who's who of children's-book illustration executed by such luminaries as Arthur Rackham, Kate Greenaway, Beatrix Potter, Edward Detmold, Edmund Dulac, Louis Wain, Arthur Timlin, Jessie M. King, Kay Nielsen, W. Heath Robinson, and Harry Clarke, some five hundred pieces in the collection all told, with prices ranging from one thousand to one hundred thousand dollars. Arranged nearby were the cream of ten thousand premier children's books, a good many of them bearing reproductions of the original pictures hanging on the walls, and they, too, were for sale, all recently acquired in one major transaction.

"This is a fabulous collection, Lou," I said to Weinstein. "Where in the world did you get it?"

"Daryl and Joan Hill," he answered, and pointed to a couple engaged in conversation on the other side of the room. Connie and I walked over and introduced ourselves.

"You're Number 108," I said to Joan Hill, recognizing her instantly.

"I am *indeed* the famous Number 108," she replied, and we both laughed.

Number 108 was the paddle number of the mystery buyer who arrived unannounced at a Swann Galleries auction in 1992 for the sale of the library of Raymond Epstein and dominated the action from start to finish, buying up lot after lot and establishing herself as someone to be reckoned with. I was so impressed that I wrote the epilogue of *A Gentle Madness* around her performance, using it as a case study of how people come and people go, but books go on forever, as

Henry Huntington so eloquently put it a century earlier. She told me then that she and her husband were just starting a collection and were "dabbling" in children's books and original illustration on the side. Dabbling, indeed; ten years later they had amassed one of the most accomplished private collections of its kind to be found in the United States. They had even set up a small business to specialize in the material, Literary Lion Books of Thousand Oaks, California, and here it all was now, passing on once again to other hands. "We've enjoyed the books and the paintings tremendously," Joan Hill said of the decision she and her husband had reached. "Now it's time to let them go."

APPENDIX
SOME THOUGHTS ON VALUE

My intention in this book has not been to suggest ways that collectors can earn a return on their investments, although I certainly have proceeded with the assumption that buying intelligently is synonymous with buying wisely, and that if at some point down the line you can sell your books for more than you paid to acquire them, so much the better. As with anything that is coveted for value, be it intrinsic or monetary, the idea is to enjoy the object for as long as it remains in your possession, and when the time comes to reach a parting of the ways, there is comfort in knowing that the separation can be made that much sweeter by the prospect of turning a tidy profit.

While it can be amusing to demonstrate how clever we have been with our book purchases during our lifetimes, it makes little sense to compare prices for comparable objects across generations. The £2,260 tendered by George Spencer, the Marquis of Blandford, at the Roxburghe sale in 1817 for a 1471 copy of Boccaccio's *Decameron* produced in Venice by Christopher Valdarfer remained the largest sum ever spent on a printed book for sixty-seven years, surpassed finally in 1884 when J. P. Morgan bought a 1459 Mainz Psalter for $24,750. When Henry Huntington outbid Joseph E. Widener for a copy of the Gutenberg Bible at the Robert Hoe sale in 1911, the hammer price of $50,000 set another record, and his thrilling victory made front-page news around the world. How much a Gutenberg Bible would sell for today is a matter of keen conjecture, but a realistic figure would probably be something on the order of $50 million, perhaps more, given the fact that only two copies remain in private hands at the time of this writing, and the prospect of any individual ever owning one gets more problematic all the time.

As interesting as these comparisons are, a study published in 1898, *Prices of Books,* described them in words that apply as much today as they did then. "The value of money has changed during each century of our history to an extent not easy to calculate with precision, because the prices of all articles have not been equally affected," Henry B. Wheatley wrote. "We can say generally that definite incomes a hundred years ago were equivalent in worth to twice their nominal amount at the present day, and that those of two hundred years ago would be worth about five times as much." Going back even further in time, Wheatley calculated that money in the fifteenth and sixteenth centuries was "worth ten or twelve times" what it was when he was writing in the late nineteenth century, and concluded with a "warning to the reader" that "a pound or a shilling in previous centuries was of more value than it is to-day, and possessed a much greater purchasing power." Wheatley wrote those words a full decade before Henry Huntington began putting together the nucleus of his great library in San Marino, California, with a total output of about $20 million spent over a period of fifteen years, a sum that today might buy a few great books, perhaps, not much more than that.

If proof of that assertion is necessary, consider the fact that when the Abel Berland copy of the First Folio of Shakespeare went up for auction at Christie's in October 2001, *advances* of $200,000 per increment were being made in the final stages of the bidding, with the final price of $6.166 million setting a record for a printed book, but not of sufficient interest, apparently, to generate so much as a paragraph of coverage in the *New York Times*. Just twelve years earlier, a New York collector had spent $2.1 million at a Sotheby's sale for a Shakespeare First Folio, and got a Second, Third, and Fourth as part of the purchase, which, like the Berland copy, was a record at the time, and that price was ten times the amount that the same copies had cost their previous owner just a decade before that. As dramatic an increase as this sounds, that kind of result was not uncommon during the frenetic decade of the 1980s, when one rule of thumb applied throughout the collectibles world was to add a zero to the cost of something purchased in the 1970s to arrive at the figure it might realize ten years later.

That said, some observations can be offered on the kind of books that most people who collect today acquire—works of fiction published during the twentieth century—and some trends can be studied that do offer food for thought. To demonstrate just how solidly the market in modern firsts has been, Allen Ahearn, the Maryland bookseller who compiles price guides of English-language first editions with his wife, Patricia, compared the prices that certain books sold for in 1980 with what they might expect to command at retail today, assuming the condition is *fine*, and an original dust jacket is present. He broke them down into two categories, those that were listed in the $50 to $200 range, and those in the $400 to $600 range.

Books selling for $50 to $200 in 1980, Their Values Now

The Brave Cowboy (New York, 1956), by Edward Abbey. $7,500.

The Sheltering Sky (London, 1949), by Paul Bowles. $4,000.

Tarzan of the Apes (Chicago, 1914), by Edgar Rice Burroughs, without dust jacket, between $5,000 and $6,000, with a jacket, $50,000. (In 1980 a copy of this exceedingly scarce book—the author's first in the Tarzan series—with a jacket would have sold for about $1,000.)

On the Road (New York, 1957), by Jack Kerouac. $5,000.

One Flew over the Cuckoo's Nest (New York, 1964), by Ken Kesey. $5,000.

The Boo (Verona, 1970), Pat Conroy's first book, self-published. $4,000.

Invisible Man (New York, 1952), by Ralph Ellison. $3,000.

Catch-22 (New York, 1961), by Joseph Heller. $4,000.

The Old Man and the Sea (New York, 1952), by Ernest Hemingway. $2,500.

The Weary Blues (New York, 1926), Langston Hughes's first book. $6,000.

Jonah's Gourd Vine (Philadelphia, 1934), Zora Neale Hurston's first book. $7,500.

To Kill a Mockingbird (Philadelphia, 1960), Harper Lee's only book, with dust jacket photo by Truman Capote. $20,000.

The Bounty Hunters (Boston, 1954), Elmore Leonard's first book. $5,000.

The Natural (New York, 1952), Bernard Malamud's first book. $5,000.

One Hundred Years of Solitude (New York, 1970), by Gabriel García Márquez, with a first issue dust jacket (an exclamation mark, not a period, at the end of the first paragraph). $3,500.

Tales of the South Pacific (New York, 1947), by James A. Michener. $4,000.

The Bluest Eye (New York, 1970), Toni Morrison's first book. $5,000.

If I Die in a Combat Zone (New York,), Tim O'Brien's first book. $2,500.

The Moviegoer (New York, 1961), Walker Percy's first book. $4,000.

The Colossus (London, 1960), Sylvia Plath's first regularly published book. $2,500.

The Bell Jar (London, 1963), by Sylvia Plath, published under the pseudonym Victoria Lucas. $5,000. The 1971 American edition, published under her real name, $200.

V (Philadelphia, 1963), Thomas Pynchon's first book, in first issue dust jacket without reviews on the back. $3,000.

The Fountainhead (Indianapolis, 1943), by Ayn Rand. $5,000.

Shane (Boston, 1949), Jack Schaefer's first book. $7,500.

If Morning Ever Comes (New York, 1964), and *The Clock Winder* (New York, 1972), the first and second novels by Anne Tyler, both now listed in dealers' catalogs in the $2,500 range.

All the King's Men (New York, 1946), by Robert Penn Warren. $5,000.

A Streetcar Named Desire (Norfolk, 1947), by Tennessee Williams. $5,000.

A Room of One's Own (London, 1929), by Virginia Woolf. $3,000.

Books Selling for $400 to $600 in 1980, Their Values Now

The Big Sleep (New York, 1939), Raymond Chandler's first book, $15,000; also *Farewell, My Lovely* (New York, 1940), his second book, $8,000, and *The High Window* (New York, 1942), his third, $6,000.

Sister Carrie (New York, 1900), Theodore Dreiser's first book. Without a dust jacket, $6,000. With a dust jacket, "it's so scarce, whatever anyone wants to put on it," according to Ahearn. "Let's say at least ten times more, $60,000."

The Waste Land (New York, 1922), by T. S. Eliot. $25,000.

The Sound and the Fury (New York, 1929), by William Faulkner. $50,000.

Tender Is the Night (New York, 1934), by F. Scott Fitzgerald. $25,000. *The Great Gatsby* (New York, 1925) was already selling for several thousand dollars in 1980 and now commands upwards of $100,000 with a dust jacket; even without a wrapper, the same book now sells for $4,500.

Casino Royale (London, 1953), Ian Fleming's first book. $30,000.

Lord of the Flies (London, 1954), by William Golding. $7,500.

Brighton Rock (New York, 1938, must say "published in June 1938"), and *A Gun for Sale* (London, 1936), both by Graham Greene, and both now routinely listed by booksellers in the $8,000 to $10,000 range.

Dune (Philadelphia, 1965), by Frank Herbert. $3,000.

Brave New World (London, 1932), by Aldous Huxley. $5,000.

Finnegan's Wake (London, 1939), by James Joyce. $4,000. Joyce's signature work, *Ulysses* (Paris, 1922), has always been an expensive book, and now sells for $75,000 or more. The first authorized American edition of the book (New York, 1934), with dust jacket, now sells for $2,500.

Call for the Dead (London, 1961), John Le Carré's first book. $10,000.

Tropic of Cancer (Paris, 1934, must state "First published September 1934"), by Henry Miller. $30,000.

When We Were Very Young (London, 1924, the first Winnie-the-Pooh book), by A. A. Milne, illustrated by Ernest H. Shepard. $7,500.

Gone with the Wind (New York, 1936, must state "Published May, 1936"), Margaret Mitchell's only book. $12,500.

The Treasure of the Sierra Madre (London, 1934), by B. Traven, the first edition in English. $7,500

Catcher in the Rye (Boston, 1951), by J. D. Salinger. $20,000.

Mrs. Dalloway (London, 1925), by Virginia Woolf. $20,000.

Books not listed in this sampling include the works by Stephen King and A. K. Rowling, primarily because both authors have followings that are uniquely their own, and sell for prices that are not reflective of the book trade. "King's books have consistently sold well, but they haven't really progressed," Ahearn said. "They had enormous jumps at the very beginning and sold for a lot of money ten or fifteen years ago, but you haven't really seen them go much beyond those levels."

The Rowling books, arriving like a comet across the sky in 1997 with the first installment in the series, *Harry Potter and the Sorcerer's Stone,* "is an anomaly in the market," Ahearn conceded, noting that the $15,000 prices demanded for books that are only a few years old defy all logic. "They continue to sell way beyond anything we've ever seen," he said. "It doesn't seem to have anything to do with anything else. I can't explain it."

SELECTED BIBLIOGRAPHY

For a comprehensive guide to the literature, history, romance, apocrypha, folklore, and mechanics of book collecting, readers are directed to the bibliographies furnished in *A Gentle Madness* (Henry Holt, 1995; Owl paperback, 1999) and *Patience & Fortitude* (HarperCollins, 2001), where my intention in both instances was to compile as thorough and varied a listing of the pastime as possible, with the latter effort meant to complement, not replicate, its forebear.

What I offer here is a decidedly truncated assortment of titles that I regard as worthwhile references for the amateur book hunter, whether it be instruction for rookies just starting out, or refresher training for veterans in need of a tune-up. The key factor is variety, with functionality and usefulness common to every selection. To provide a sense of contrast, a number of the older primers—easily recognizable by their years of publication—have been included to provide perspective and continuity. Though a few of the books cited are out of print, most can be found in all good libraries, or are readily available for purchase at reasonable prices in the secondhand market through such on-line search engines as www.abebooks.com, www.addall.com, and www.bookfinder.com. It bears stressing that this is by no means a definitive list; it merely represents the items that I would recommend for inclusion on any syllabus for a nuts-and-bolts course on the elements of book collecting, if I were asked. Happy hunting.

Ahearn, Allen and Patricia. *Book Collecting 2000: A Comprehensive Guide.* New York: G. P. Putnam's, 2000.
This compendium of solid advice is part of a series (see also 1989 and 1995 editions) issued by the Ahearns apart from their price compilations, and includes a lot of sensible material, especially in the areas of comparison shopping on the Internet, the pseudonyms of authors, and details on how to determine the first editions of British and American publishers.

———. *Collected Books: The Guide to Values 2002 Edition.* New York: G. P. Putnam's Sons, 2001. (See also 1991 and 1998 editions.)
These comprehensive guides feature current price values culled from numerous sources, with issue points enumerated where appropriate, and were begun as the successors to Van Allan Bradley's highly successful series of guides, *Handbook of Values* (New York: G. P. Putnam's, 1972, 1975, 1978, 1982), which are worth owning in their own right. The 2002 edition includes an appendix offering a thorough listing of bibliographies devoted to the writings of individual authors.

American Book Prices Current. (1895–). Washington, CT: Bancroft-Parkman, Inc. (The most recent volume is 107, covering September 2000–August 2001. For complete ordering information, see www.bookpricescurrent.com.)
The printed volumes of this periodical, bound in bright-red cloth, constitute a cumulative record of prices realized at auction in the antiquarian book trade over a period of time that embraces all of the

twentieth century, and then some. The CD-ROM version, with updates furnished annually, is inclusive from 1975 on. This latter option has the advantage of an every-word index that allows for the searching of some remarkably arcane categories (all books sold at auction with the words "photography" or "slavery" in the title, for example, or books bound in black velvet or human skin, any books with the name of a person in the title—i.e., *Billy Budd, Billy Phelan's Greatest Game, Anything for Billy, Charming Billy, The Collected Works of Billy the Kid*). Copies can be found in the reference rooms of major libraries, and individual copies turn up from time to time in the antiquarian market. ABPC, as this bibliographical institution is known, is about as vital a guide as there is for determining value. (See chapters 4 and 7 for the author's interviews with Katharine Leab.)

Arnold, William Harris. *Ventures in Book Collecting.* New York and London: Charles Scribner's Sons, 1923.

The perspectives in this entertaining rumination are those of a prominent American collector, not a dealer, which is typically the case in a book like this; making it doubly interesting is the erudite foreword offered by Thomas J. Wise, written ten years before his fall from grace as the notorious forger of "certain nineteenth century pamphlets."

Blanck, Jacob. *Bibliography of American Literature.* 9 vols. (Compiled for the Bibliographical Society of America.) New Haven, CT: Yale University Press, 1955–1991.

A monumental inventory of the literary canon of American literature embracing the period of the Revolution to about 1930, BAL provides nearly forty thousand records of the literary works of approximately three hundred authors. Regrettably, not all nine volumes are in print, making the acquisition of a complete set difficult and expensive, but all good libraries do have copies. If ever a reference work cried out for a CD-ROM edition, this is it, although two guides to BAL, *A Selective Index* and an *Epitome*, both compiled by Michael Winship with Philip B. Eppard and Rachel J. Howarth (Golden, CO: North American Press, 1995), are superb guides to the wealth of data it contains.

Bowers, Fredson, with an introduction by G. Thomas Tanselle. *Principles of Bibliographical Description.* New Castle, DE: Oak Knoll Press, 1994. (Reissue of the 1949 edition.)
G. Thomas Tanselle, an influential bibliographer in his own right, calls this book "one of the indisputable classics of twentieth-century scholarship." It is the standard guide to descriptive bibliography over the past half century, and certain to maintain that distinction for years to come. A densely packed volume of more than five hundred pages, this is the means by which one learns how to "deal" with a book in all its parts, and comes as close to indispensability as any single reference can hope to achieve.

Bruccoli, Matthew J., general editor. *First Printings of American Authors: Contributions Toward Descriptive Checklists.* 5 vols. Detroit: Bruccoli Clark/Gale Research Co., 1977–1987.
These oversized books represented an important contribution to the study of what its title suggests, the *first* printings of selected American authors, and compiled them in their initial appearances in American and English editions. The striking innovation was the facsimile reproduction of selected copyright pages and dust jacket covers.

Carter, John. *A B C for Book Collectors.* Seventh edition, revised with corrections and additions by Nicolas Barker. New Castle, DE: Oak Knoll Press, 1992.
Collectors of books about books will certainly want to have the first edition of this classic on their shelves (New York: Alfred A. Knopf, 1952), but Barker's revision, with numerous updates, fixes, and amendments, is by far the superior version, and the one recommended for its utility. The beauty of this encyclopedic gathering of

450 book terms, many of them reflecting Carter's droll sense of humor, is that it has been around now for fifty years, constantly proving its worth.

Carter, John. *Taste and Technique in Book Collecting*. Cambridge, England: Cambridge University Press, 1948. (Reissued by Private Libraries Association, London, 1970.)
A bit on the esoteric side, occasionally tedious, and clearly intended for the advanced collector, but a respected survey of changing trends and practices at midcentury that ought to be perused at some point by those seriously engaged in the pursuit, if only cursorily.

Carter, John, and Percy H. Muir, editors. *Printing and the Mind of Man: The Impact of Print on Five Centuries of Western Civilization*. London: Cassell and Co./New York: Holt, Rinehart and Winston, 1967. (Reprint, Munich: Karl Pressler, 1983.)
The descriptive catalog of any major book exhibition is worth taking a good look at, with this one being the prototypical example of the genre. The 424 books included in the landmark London show mounted in 1963 were chosen for "the ideas they brought to the world for the first time, and are of prime importance" to humanity. The individual commentaries on the books, and the bibliographical references, are superb.

De Halsalle, Henry. *The Romance of Modern First Editions*. Philadelphia: J. B. Lippincott, 1931.
What is especially interesting about this book is that it was written during the depths of the Great Depression, yet even then the ebullient author seemed intent on recommending recently published books almost certain to appreciate in monetary value; the title of the British edition, in fact, was *Treasure Trove in Book Land*. Among his tips that have held up: "Henry James is decidedly worth buying at his present low prices," along with strong endorsements for Oscar Wilde and Joseph Conrad. His wild enthusiasm for the poet Francis Thompson,

on the other hand ("bears the unmistakable stamp of greatness"), demonstrates just how fickle the concept of literary fashion can be.

Connolly, Cyril. *The Modern Movement: A Discussion of 100 Books from England, France and America 1880–1950.* New York: Atheneum, 1966.

Of lists there is no end, but this one is of continuing importance, and one that should be in the working vocabulary of every collector of books generally regarded to be *modern* (a genre of fiction that emerged full-blown in the early twentieth century, and is not to be confused with *contemporary* writing, which applies to anything of recent vintage, or even *modern first editions,* which has become synonymous with fiction of the last half century.) Cyril Connolly was a hugely influential British critic of the mid-twentieth century, and his top one hundred remain a force to this day. "I have tried to choose books with outstanding originality and richness of texture and with the spark of rebellion alight, books which aspire to be works of art," he explained. "Realism is not enough."

Feather, John. *A Dictionary of Book History.* New York: Oxford University Press, 1986.

This one-volume alphabetical reference of 650 entries, gathered by an English professor whose vita includes extensive experience in both the book trade and library science, covers a number of intersecting disciplines, bibliography, history of printing, libraries, and collecting, foremost among them. One example of its wide-ranging bookishness is to be found on two entries that appear on facing pages, one for *Cambridge University Press,* the academic publisher established in 1520, the other for the word *cancel,* a term describing a leaf that has been removed from a sheet after printing, or a leaf subsequently inserted to replace it.

Haller, Margaret. *The Book Collector's Fact Book.* New York: Arco Publishing Co., 1976.

This glossary takes a somewhat similar approach to that of Carter's *A B C for Book Collectors,* but does not duplicate it. There is some overlap, but this is a worthwhile companion, especially since it was designed with the collector of "moderate means" in mind.

Gascoigne, Bamber. *How to Identify Prints: A Complete Guide to Manual and Mechanical Processes from Woodcut to Ink-Jet.* New York: Thames and Hudson, 1986.

Is it an *etching* or an *engraving*? If it is the latter, is it *copper, wood,* or *steel*? What are *relief, intaglio,* and *planographic* types of print? Knowing your way around graphic art is like money in the bank for the modern collector; those who constantly despair over trying how to determine exactly *what* a print is have all the help they need in this richly illustrated volume.

Johnson, Merle. *American First Editions,* 4th ed., revised and enlarged by Jacob Blanck. New York: R. R. Bowker, 1942. (1st ed. 1928, 2nd ed. 1932, 3rd ed. 1936.)

It was Merle Johnson who popularized the phrase "high spots" with an influential book released in 1929, *High Spots of American Literature,* which led him to produce more comprehensive compilations, and which led his successor, Jacob Blanck, in turn, to embark on *Bibliography of American Literature.* Though largely superseded by that massive undertaking, *American First Editions* still has its uses, including listings of books by authors who were not included in BAL; a good item to pick up if you see it in a secondhand shop, and if the price is right.

Matthews, Jack. *Collecting Rare Books for Pleasure and Profit.* New York: G. P. Putnam's Sons, 1977.

The agenda here is to regard books as investments, with emphasis on modern firsts, private presses, association copies, and the validation of issue points; a good bibliography and index.

Muir, P. H. *Book-Collecting as a Hobby.* New York: Alfred A. Knopf, 1947.
Written as a series of letters to "Everyman," the greatly admired British bookseller Percy Muir weighed in here with a graceful interpretation of exactly what it is that makes a collector. "It is less a matter of money than of method," he reminded his readers, requiring them to begin with a plan. There is a good humor throughout, and I especially like the chapter "How to Transform Mountains into Molehills," where there is this nugget: "Book-collectors sometimes feel almost as completely beyond human aid." He offers sage advice on how to seek help.

Peters, Jean, editor. *Book Collecting: A Modern Guide.* New York: R. R. Bowker, 1977.
A collection of twelve essays on such subjects as bookseller relations, auctions, the antiquarian market, manuscripts, descriptive bibliography, forgeries, care and condition, appraisals, collection organization, the literature of book collecting. Contributors include G. Thomas Tanselle, Lola L. Szladits, Terry Belanger, and Robert A. Wilson.

————. *Collectible Books: Some New Paths.* New York: R. R. Bowker, 1979.
More of the same as above, nine essays dealing variously with collectible books that are *non-firsts,* books in series, book catalogs, American fiction since 1960, film books, mass-market paperbacks, photography as book illustration, and trade bindings; William B. Todd, Daniel J. Leab, William P. Barlow Jr., Stuart Bennett, and Peter B. Howard are among the contributors.

Rendell, Kenneth W. *History Comes to Life: Collecting Historical Letters and Documents.* Norman, OK: University of Oklahoma Press, 1995.
Letters, autographs, and handwritten documents—manuscript collecting is the first cousin to book-collecting—is discussed by one

of the world's leading dealers in the field, with material of interest in all subject areas, and all historical periods. A major authority in authenticating originals, Rendell has much to share on the subject of spotting fraudulent material.

Rickards, Maurice. *Collecting Printed Ephemera.* New York: Abbeville Press, 1988.

Valentines, postcards, menus, broadsides, posters, theater programs, ferry tickets, railroad timetables, all are similar in that they are printed items meant to be discarded after accomplishing their intended function. The author of this comprehensive survey founded the Ephemera Society in London in 1975, and served as editor of *The Ephemerist,* the leading journal in the field; this authoritative reference has hundreds of superb illustrations.

Schreyer, Alice D., editor. *Rare Books 1983–1984: Trends, Collections, Sources.* New York: R. R. Bowker, 1984.

This anthology of superb essays by a number of eminent authorities from all sectors of the rare-book world was published at the very time that prices for collectibles were taking off with white-hot enthusiasm for all things rare and beautiful; an excellent reference that brims with material of continuing relevance.

Slater, J. H. *How to Collect Books.* London: George Bell and Sons, 1905.

This is one of the earliest attempts to romanticize collecting as an undertaking that anyone, not just the wealthy, can enjoy, offering tips on how to proceed within budgetary limitations; it includes some wonderful illustrations to boot.

Stewart, Seumas. *Book Collecting: A Beginner's Guide.* New York: E. P. Dutton, 1973.

The focus of this thorough study by a London bookseller is in troubleshooting "problems" that crop up in the evaluation of first editions. I especially like the advice of John Fleming, given in the foreword: "A rule one must remember: Examine and collate. Examine and collate again. Make sure your purchase is perfect. Even if you become a seasoned collector, don't take the word of anyone."

Storm, Colton, and Howard Peckham. *Invitation to Book Collecting: Its Pleasures and Practices.* New York: R. R. Bowker, 1947.
A first-rate introduction to the pastime as it was undergoing philosophical changes in the immediate aftermath of World War II, and predicated on this memorable turn-of-phrase: "The perfect definition of rare books is as elusive as the nest of the bristle-thighed curlew; neither has been found."

Streeter, Thomas Winthrop. *The Celebrated Collection of Americana Formed by the Late Thomas Winthrop Streeter.* 7 vols. New York: Parke-Bernet Galleries, 1966–1969. (Index compiled by Edward J. Lazare, 1970.)
By far some of the most worthwhile information available to the book hunter is to be found in the catalogs of important auctions. The Streeter sale—in the field of Americana second in importance only to the great dispersal of George Brinley in the 1800s—produced seven remarkable volumes itemizing a collection of four thousand items in every conceivable area. I acquired my set in 1990 at the Sotheby's sale of another great collector, the late H. Bradley Martin.

Taylor, Archer, revised and corrected by William P. Barlow Jr. *Book Catalogues: Their Varieties and Uses.* New Castle, DE: Oak Knoll Press, 1986. (1st ed. 1957.)
This wonderfully accessible gateway into the world of bibliography for "civilians" delivers an appreciation for exactly what it is a book catalog has to offer, be it one produced by a dealer or an auction house. The reprint is published, incidentally, by the leading publisher of books about books in North America (www.oakknoll.com).

Uden, Grant. *Understanding Book-Collecting.* London: Baron Publishing Co., 1995. (Reprint of the 1982 edition.)

A sophisticated, handsomely illustrated overview that employs an historical approach to explaining the technical aspects of collecting. A nice touch is the appendix with a clever learning aid to help master the use of roman numerals, a useful device to have around when trying to determine the copyright date of so many books published prior to the twentieth century.

Wheatley, Henry B. *Prices of Books: An Inquiry into the Changes in the Price of Books Which Have Occurred in England at Different Periods.* London: George Allen, 1898.

The thrust of this little gem of a book is amply summarized by the subtitle, to which I add my admiration for the delightfully anecdotal approach its author takes to the subject, and the obvious command he has of the material. Price, in his lexicon, is a murky concept, with ramifications that often "partake more of an archaeological, than of a practical character."

Wilson, Robert A. *Modern Book Collecting.* New York: Alfred A. Knopf, 1980. (Reprint: Lyons & Burford, 1992.)

Now more than twenty years old, this is still the best primer for beginners who plan to buy what are generically known as *modern first editions,* a field that probably applies to most book collectors today. Respected as the owner of the legendary Phoenix Book Shop in New York, Robert Wilson brought a keen sense of the market to his examination, and his sections on author bibliographies and ways to determine if books are first editions make the work must-reading in its own right.

Zempel, Edward N., and Linda A. Verkler, editors. 4th ed. *First Editions: A Guide to Identification.* Peoria, IL: Spoon River Press, 2001. (1st ed. 1977, 2nd ed. 1989, 3rd ed. 1995.)

This is by far the most detailed assembly of statements obtained from North American, British Commonwealth, and Irish trade and academic publishers on methods that have been used to designate first editions on their copyright pages, comprising, in the latest version, some forty-two hundred publishing houses, and incorporating the compilations of H. S. Boutell, whose *First Editions of To-day and How to Tell Them* were staple bibliographical tools of the 1920s and 1930s.

INDEX

Index

Index

About the Author

Nicholas Basbanes is the author of *A Gentle Madness* and *Patience & Fortitude*. He lives in North Grafton, Massachusetts.